Stadium Stories:

Denver Broncos

Stadium Stories™ Series

Stadium Stories:

Denver Broncos

Colorful Tales of the Orange and Blue

Larry Zimmer

The Globe Pequot Press

GUILFORD, CONNECTICUT

Stadium Stories is a trademark of Morris Book Publishing, LLC.

Text design: Casey Shain
Cover photos (clockwise from top left): Rich Clarkson and Associates, Rich Clarkson and Associates, David Gonzales/Rich Clarkson and Associates, Ryan McKee/Rich Clarkson and Associates, Rich Clarkson and Associates, Ryan McKee/Rich Clarkson and Associates

Library of Congress Cataloging-in-Publication Data
Zimmer, Larry.
    Stadium stories : Denver Broncos : colorful tales of the orange and blue / Larry Zimmer.—1st ed.
        p. cm. — (Stadium stories series)
    ISBN 0-7627-2766-7
  1. Denver Broncos (Football team) I. Title: Denver Broncos. II. Title. III. Series.
    GV956.D37Z56 2004
    796.332'64'0978883—dc22   2004042547

Manufactured in the United States of America
First Edition/First Printing

I would like to dedicate this book to four people:

First, to the two biggest Broncos fans I know; my son, Larry, who has never missed a Broncos Super Bowl game, and has created a Broncos shrine in his office at LBL Enterprises, despite being in the middle of Seahawk territory in Seattle; and my son-in-law, J. C. Robb, who has missed few Broncos games in recent memory (my daughter, Tracey, and granddaughter, Shannon, tolerate his addiction).

To my loyal producer, Jerry Peters, who has been by my side for more than 20 years of my broadcasting career.

And to my wife, Brigitte, my best friend, most loyal supporter, biggest critic, and partner in my sports broadcasts. As my spotter, there is no more dedicated worker in the booth.

Contents

Introduction

I spent twenty-six years behind the microphone painting a word picture of the Denver Broncos for the best fans in professional football.

I will never forget November 19, 1995. That was the day I broadcast my 500th Bronco game. Denver beat the San Diego Chargers 30–27 in another come-from-behind victory. I have two "game balls" from that day. One is a ceremonial game ball presented in pregame ceremonies. The other is one of my most treasured possessions: a real ball that was used in the game and signed by coach Mike Shanahan and all of the players who played a significant role in the Broncos win.

For the first nineteen years of my career, I was the color commentator with Bob Martin, and the team of Martin and Zimmer became popular and synonymous with Broncos football. When Bob passed away in 1990, I stepped into the play-by-play role and had seven exciting years with Dave Logan. Logan is a legend in Colorado high school circles, and I'd broadcasted every game that he played at the University of Colorado. Dave had a fine NFL career with the Cleveland Browns and finished with the Broncos. There is continuity in the broadcasts, because when I stepped away from the microphone after the 1996 season, Dave took over as the play-by-play voice and continues in that role today.

I've had a couple of occasions to return to the booth on some preseason games, and I was invited back to do a quarter for the final game played in Mile High Stadium on December 23, 2000.

Bob Martin and I had some great years. When I joined him in 1971, the Broncos had never had a winning season, and the first one was still two years away. We were together for Denver's "Miracle Season" in 1977. We watched the Broncos become an American Football Conference powerhouse with three more conference championships in the late 1980s, but they were always a bridesmaid in the Super Bowl.

With regret I had to broadcast the Super Bowl in 1990, while Bob watched from a hospital room in New Orleans. He was battling cancer, and it got the best of him just days before the big game. He died a few weeks later.

The Broncos franchise is unique. It was founded on a shoestring, was a laughing stock in the early years, and almost had the last rites read on a couple of occasions. Yet it has endured, becoming one of professional football's most respected franchises. The Broncos have had many "firsts." The Broncos played the first American Football League game in 1960. The Broncos are the only team to borrow a quarterback from another team for one season. (It was Jacky Lee from Houston in 1964.) The Broncos were the first AFL team to beat an NFL team, not once, but twice in a row. The Broncos had the first black quarterback, Marlin Briscoe. When the NFL adopted the sudden death overtime rule in 1974, the first overtime game was played by the Broncos and Pittsburgh Steelers. Oddly enough, neither team scored in overtime, and it ended 35–35. In 1987 the Broncos were part of the only time there were two games on Monday night. The game with the Vikings at the Hubert Humphrey Dome was moved from Sunday to Monday night because of the seventh game of the World Series, when the Twins beat the Cardinals in the same arena. The winningest quarterback in NFL history, John Elway, wore the orange and blue of the Denver Broncos. Not many announcers have the opportunity to watch a player like John Elway each week. I was blessed.

Until John Elway's 2004 induction into the Pro Football Hall of Fame in Canton, Ohio, the only entry from the Denver Broncos was a vertically striped sock that unfortunately defined the team as the laughing stock of pro football in the early years. The sock hangs next to a picture of a 1960 game with the Houston Oilers that shows Billy Cannon running the ball against the Broncos, who were wearing those socks. Cannon, the All-American from LSU, became a prize catch of the brand new American Football League. The plate under the sock in the Hall reads:

> *Heisman Trophy winner Billy Cannon signed with the Houston Oilers for 1960! Meanwhile, the Denver Broncos were playing in second-hand uniforms made famous by the vertically-striped socks that were later burned in a public ceremony. Thus, the AFL's great hope and its early futility are graphically portrayed as Cannon gains yardage against the Denver team.*

In the pages that follow, I have tried to capture the flavor of the Denver Broncos—the team, the personalities, and the drama that I have witnessed over the years.

The Early Years: A Decade of Futility

The Broncos, born in 1960, were conceived a year earlier. Lamar Hunt was unsuccessful in landing a National Football League franchise to move to Dallas and set out to form a new league. The twenty-six-year-old millionaire oilman had two things going for him: determination and money. He convinced a Houston oilman, K. S. "Bud" Adams, to join him and the American Football League was off and running.

At the same time things were happening in Denver that didn't involve football. The minor league baseball franchise, owned and operated by Bob Howsam, was quite successful. Later, Howsam would become a baseball icon as general manager of the St. Louis Cardinals and president of the Cincinnati Reds.

Howsam grew up in Colorado, and following his navy stint in World War II, he was brought into baseball as secretary of the Western League by his father-in-law, the legendary three-term governor and later United States Senator, Edwin C. "Big Ed" Johnson. Howsam, with the help of his father, Lee, and brother, Earl, bought one of the Western League teams, the Denver Bears, for $75,000. Howsam made a new ball park a priority, getting the land and the financing to build Bears Stadium.

While Hunt and Adams were hatching the idea of another major football league, the same thing was happening in baseball. The Giants and Dodgers had vacated New York City for the West Coast in 1958, and millionaire lawyer and sports fan William Shea wanted to bring baseball back to Gotham. Shea hired innovative baseball executive Branch Rickey to help him launch the Continental Baseball League. The goal was for the new league to gain major league status in three to five years.

Howsam had gained the attention of baseball people with his successful management of the Bears, now a Triple A franchise. He was twice named Minor League Executive of the Year. When he was offered a franchise in the proposed new league, Howsam didn't blink. His quick answer was "yes." Although he didn't realize it, things were set in motion that would bring Denver major league status in football thirty-three years before it would achieve that status in baseball.

When Hunt and Adams offered Howsam a spot in the AFL, he also accepted, reasoning that a football team would keep the stadium busy for nine months a year.

Howsam was in over his head financially and today laughs about his audacity. His family was comfortable, but they were certainly not millionaires. The father and two sons had scraped together money to buy the Bears in 1948 and had sold personal bonds to build the stadium. Although the baseball franchise was successful, it certainly didn't produce the kind of revenue needed to get a new franchise in a new league off the ground. Yet, Howsam found himself doing just that in not one, but two different sports.

If this were a Hollywood script instead of a real life story, it would have a happy ending. But for the Howsams, it didn't.

The Continental League was announced on July 29, 1959. Two weeks later, August 14, 1959, Howsam joined Hunt,

Adams, and Hilton in Chicago to announce the formation of the American Football League, which would begin play in the fall of 1960.

The wheels came off the Continental League quickly. Major League Baseball's reserve clause, binding even minor league players to one team, made it impossible for the new league to sign players. To satisfy Shea the major league moguls expanded into New York and Houston. The New York franchise would play in a new stadium to be built on Long Island, later named Shea Stadium. William Shea's dream of bringing a team back to New York had been realized and he lost interest in the Continental League. It died without a game being played or a player signed.

Howsam's first love was baseball and now his dream was dashed. Construction was well underway on a stadium addition, and all he had was a minor league baseball team and a football team with no name, no organization, no coach, and no players.

The National Football League didn't take the end of its monopoly sitting down. After failing to induce Hunt and Adams to drop the AFL in return for expansion franchises, the NFL announced on January 28, 1960, that it would expand into Dallas and Minneapolis-Saint Paul. Another Texas millionaire oilman, Clint Murchison Jr., was awarded the Dallas franchise to directly confront Hunt's Dallas Texans. The Twin Cities franchise went to the same group that earlier had committed to the AFL. Two days after Minnesota joined the NFL, that AFL franchise was awarded to Oakland instead.

It should be noted that while the AFL did survive, the Texans did not in Dallas. After playing three seasons in the antiquated Cotton Bowl, it became obvious to Hunt that Dallas-Fort Worth couldn't support his team, and the

Cowboys, who were playing in the brand new Texas Stadium. Hunt moved to Kansas City and still owns and operates the highly successful Chiefs organization.

Howsam purchased temporary stands that would be erected on the east side of the stadium, increasing the capacity for football to 35,000.

The team was named "Broncos" in a statewide contest.

Denver's first general manager was forty-five-year-old Dean Griffing. Howsam was attracted to him because he had a reputation for being extremely frugal, while still building successful teams. Griffing spent his career as player, coach, and general manager in the Canadian Football League. His most recent successes had been with the Saskatchewan Rough Riders.

Neither Howsam nor Griffing were familiar with American college football, so they conducted the team's first draft using college football guides. Other owners had millions to offer their draft choices and in many cases were successful. Howsam only had debts.

Griffing didn't have to build an organization. He was the organization. The team needed a training site, equipment, uniforms, and most importantly, a coach. He looked north-ward to Canada and on January 1, 1960, hired former NFL quarterback and coach of the Rough Riders, Frank Filchock.

Filchock's familiarity with Canadian talent was good for Denver. The man who replaced him as interim coach for the final six games of the 1959 season, after Filchock was fired, was also the Rough Riders quarterback, Frank Tripucka.

Griffing and Filchock convinced the former Notre Dame quarterback to join them as a player-coach. Tripucka wanted to coach but agreed to be on the active roster while developing two young quarterbacks. Before that first preseason was over, the two young quarterbacks were gone and Tripucka was the man. In that inaugural season in 1960, Tripucka completed 52 percent of his passes for 3,038 yards and twenty-four touchdowns. He was the starting quarterback through 1963, making the AFL All-Star Game in 1962, when he led the Broncos to a 7–7 season. He is still their fourth all-time quarterback in passing yardage, with 7,676 yards. He set the single-game passing record of 447 yards against Buffalo in 1962, and the mark stood for thirty-eight years. John Elway came within 15 yards of the mark, Charlie Johnson came within 2 yards, but the record was surpassed in 2000 by reserve quarterback Gus Frerotte, who passed for 462 yards against San Diego. Tripucka's number (18) is one of three retired Broncos numbers. He was an original inductee into the Broncos Ring of Fame in 1986.

The original Broncos had three assistant coaches. Today, the Broncos have a staff of twenty-one coaches and fourteen others in football operations and scouting. This small staff got eighty players under contract, some as a result of public tryouts. Amazingly, some quality players were signed. Austin "Goose" Gonsoulin was passed over in the NFL draft after a fine college career at Baylor. He came to Denver and starred at safety for seven seasons. Before he completed his Denver career, Gonsoulin was the all-time AFL leader in interceptions with forty-three, a number still good for the second spot in Bronco history. In the inaugural 1960 season he had eleven interceptions, still on top of Denver's record book, and was an original inductee into the Broncos Ring of Fame.

The original Broncos uniforms came from a defunct college football all-star game in Tucson called the Copper Bowl. The jerseys were what Griffing called "gold." The players called the color "mustard yellow." The pants and

Despite Denver's bargain basement operation, the team had two outstanding offensive players: quarterback Frank Tripucka (18) and wide receiver Lionel Taylor (87). They established records that lasted into the 1990s. (Courtesy Rich Clarkson and Associates)

helmets were brown. Griffing found a sporting goods store that was trying to unload some old socks that had vertical stripes. Griffing made a deal.

Those were the only uniforms the Broncos had. They wore them at home and on the road. Were the players embarrassed to dress in those uniforms? "Hell yes," said former player Frank Bernardi. "They certainly didn't build confidence."

After the Broncos won that famous first AFL game on September 9, 1960, 13–10 over the Boston Patriots, the team stayed in the east for games two and three. Bears baseball prevented them from playing at home, and it was cheaper to stay put rather than make the round trips to Denver. They practiced in Tripucka's home town of Plainfield, New Jersey.

Denver won in Buffalo, and with a 2–0 record the players were a happy lot as they returned to their eastern headquarters to prepare for game three against the New York Titans, which they lost. The AFL also was off to a good start, particularly with a television contract with ABC. Television audiences grew as the nation's fans took to the wide-open, high-scoring games.

After three games on the road, the Broncos came home and staged an inaugural parade down 16th Street in Denver. It was largely ignored. Photos of the event show a few people standing at the curb wondering what it was all about. Newspaper ads proclaimed October 2, 1960, "Pro Football Sunday." North and South Stands tickets were on sale for $3.50. Sideline seats on the east and west sides went for $4.50. Season tickets were $24.50 and $31.50, respectively. Two thousand-five hundred had been sold.

Bears Stadium was half full (18,372) for the first home game against the Oakland Raiders. Those fans went home happy as the Broncos pushed their record to 3–1 with a 31–14 win. The Broncos started 4–2, but they wouldn't win again in 1960.

The First Training Camp—More Like Boot Camp

One of the original Broncos was Frank Bernardi, who played defensive back for the Chicago Cardinals for five seasons, after a fine college career at Colorado. Bernardi said, "The Cardinals were the shakiest franchise in the NFL, so I thought I'd give the Broncos and the new league a try. I really had no idea what I was getting into. The Cardinals had financial problems, but we had first-class facilities and first-class travel."

The first Broncos training camp was at Colorado School of Mines in suburban Golden. They were housed on the top floor of an old campus building. It was one big open room. Bernardi remembers, "We slept on army surplus cots, covered with army surplus blankets, and hung our clothes on long pipes. There were no partitions and we had common bathroom facilities. Our training table was at the school cafeteria and we went through the line with the students. We really didn't get enough to eat and as soon as the meal was over we headed to downtown Golden to get a pizza.

"On the field," Bernardi said, "things were not very well organized. We designed things on the fly. It didn't seem to matter. We had so much experience on the team that the coaches didn't have a lot of coaching to do. It was sort of ragtag. What made it tolerable was that we had fun. We griped a lot, but we still had fun."

Hey, Look What We Found in a Touch Football Game

While working out in New Jersey, a defensive back from New Mexico Highlands University, who had appeared in eight games in 1959 with the Chicago Bears, showed up at the camp. In a touch football game after practice, Frank Tripucka observed that he caught all the passes thrown to him and talked Frank Filchock into allowing the player to run some patterns on offense. Lionel Taylor's career as a wide receiver was born. He started the next game against New York and finished the 1960 season with 92 receptions for 1,235 yards and 12 touchdowns and was selected to the All-AFL team, a feat he repeated in 1961 and 1965. He was the leading receiver in the AFL for five of the first six years of the league's existence and never caught fewer than seventy-six passes in a season. Only in recent years have some of his receiving records been surpassed. Taylor was one of the original inductees into the Broncos Ring of Fame in 1984.

The team's financial losses were too much for Howsam. He put the Broncos and Bears up for sale, and by the spring of 1961 he had a firm offer from a group that would have moved both teams to San Antonio.

Denver businessman Calvin Kunz convinced another minority owner, Gerald Phipps, to make an effort to buy the franchises so they would stay in Denver. Phipps later said that the determining factor for him was the Bears. He didn't want to see Denver without baseball. He said he was so-so about the football team, but once it completed a season, it wouldn't look good for the city to lose the franchise. Phipps became the largest single stockholder and brought his brother Allan, an attorney, into the organization, which was incorporated as Rocky Mountain Empire Sports.

The Phipps brothers were faced with saving the Broncos for Denver twice more. In 1965 Kunz decided to recoup his losses and made a secret move that created a "voting trust" with other Empire Sports stockholders who wanted out. He gained control of 52 percent of the stock without including the Phipps brothers. Gerry and Allan rallied support against the "trust," which was entertaining offers from out-of-town interests that would move the team to Atlanta. Their efforts were successful.

Phipps had to rally the citizens yet again after the AFL merged with the NFL. The AFL had driven up salaries, there were lawsuits, and the league had a new five-year television contract with NBC. The NFL ended its battle with the young league on June 8,1966, by announcing a merger that would gradually be completed by the 1970 season. The champions of the two leagues would meet for a pro football championship and teams from the two leagues would begin playing each other during the preseason of 1967.

In 1963, thirty-four-year-old Jack Faulkner, a protégé of legendary coach Sid Gillman, became head coach. He dumped the brown and gold uniforms, changing the colors to orange and blue, and organized a public burning of the vertically striped socks. Now, despite the lack of success on the field, the fans had started their love affair with the Broncos. They were buying tickets. The merger agreement required each team to have a stadium with 50,000 seats. Bears Stadium had 34,000, so wheels were set in motion that ultimately led to an expanded stadium. Lou Saban, who had won an AFL championship at Buffalo, took over December 19, 1966, as coach and general manager, and lobbied for a new home for the team. The headquarters was a Quonset hut a few blocks

The Broncos franchise gained stability when Gerald Phipps gained control in the late 1960s. Here he congratulates running back Otis Armstrong. (Courtesy Rich Clarkson and Associates)

If You're on the Can, Watch Out for the Hand

The Quonset hut was misleading. It had a square false front, but inside the roof was rounded on the sides and you had to watch your head.

Longtime Bronco assistant coach Stan Jones (he served under Lou Saban, John Ralston, Red Miller, and Dan Reeves) came with Saban from Maryland. He remembers that one of the problems was in the restroom. "The wall curved in," he said, "and when you sat on the commode there, you had to tilt to your right a little bit. The coffee machine was inside the door and people would reach in to pour a cup of coffee. I said, 'This is pro football?'"

The practice field was also a problem. Situated between the offices and the stadium, it wasn't a full field—not long enough, nor wide enough. One side dropped off to an embankment that went down to a parking lot. Coaches and players alike laughed about wide receivers running routes, forgetting where they were, falling off the field, and rolling down the embankment.

from Bears Stadium. Phipps found land north of Denver, in suburban Adams County, and constructed practice fields and a building housing a modern locker room, an up-to-date training room, and an equipment room. The Broncos moved into their new digs on March 1, 1967. With one expansion in the late 1970s, it would be their home for twenty-three years and four days, when they moved into their current Dove Valley headquarters in 1993. Saban got his new practice facility and signed his top draft choice in 1967, Syracuse running back Floyd Little. He was the first top draft choice to sign with the Broncos.

It's not too often that preseason games are taken seriously, but in the summer of 1967 all eyes were on the games that for the first time put AFL teams on the same field with NFL teams. Leave it to the Broncos to make history. They played the Detroit Lions and Minnesota Vikings on successive Saturday nights at the University of Denver Stadium. The 21,228 fans who showed up to watch the Lions slaughter the Broncos instead saw an inspired Denver squad become the first AFL team to beat an NFL team. Final score: Denver 13, Detroit 7. Veteran Detroit defensive tackle Alex Karras had boasted, "If we lose to the Denver Broncos, I'll walk back to Detroit." He didn't, but Denver radio stations spoofed all week as they followed his progress back to the Motor City. The next week against the Vikings, an additional 10,500 fans showed up to see if Saban's team was for real. Final score: Denver 14, Minnesota 3.

A few years later, the fans tired of Saban and his tenure was doomed with the first game of 1971, when the Broncos passed up a chance to beat the powerful Miami Dolphins and settled for a tie. Saban said afterward that "half-a-loaf was better than none." The fans became hostile; Saban sunk into depression and resigned.

In 1972 Phipps turned to the college ranks and hired Stanford's John Ralston, who just days before had won his second straight Rose Bowl by beating Michigan, having beaten Ohio State the year before.

The Denver Broncos were about to enter a new era. They had played twelve seasons without being over .500. They had survived crisis after crisis. Under Ralston they would achieve that first winning season and set their sights on football's biggest prize—the Super Bowl.

Floyd Little—A Homicidal Maniac with Bowlegs

L ong after the aspen leaves have turned golden and dropped from the trees and winter begins to grip the Rocky Mountains, football is still being played. Games in December are played on a surreal stage. At kickoff time the afternoon is sunny and crisp, but it soon gives way to shadows, and as darkness falls the lights take over and a misty haze develops as a result of the rapid drop in temperature. This was the backdrop of one of the most dramatic moments in the history of Mile High Stadium, a scene I vividly recall: With the mist forming a scrim in front of the stage, number 44 is lifted to the shoulders of his Bronco teammates and carried to the sidelines. Floyd Little has played his final game, ending a brilliant nine-year career.

What a finish it was. A Hollywood writer couldn't have written it better. Little was tired—physically and mentally he had paid the price. He had led Denver to its first-ever winning season in 1973, when the team came within one win of making the playoffs. The Broncos followed that with a second winning season in 1974, but Little was no longer the main man. Denver had used the number one draft choice in 1973 to

Floyd Little is carried from the field by the fans after his final game at Mile High Stadium. (Courtesy Eric Lars Bakke)

take running back Otis Armstrong, Purdue's Big Ten rushing champion. In Armstrong's second year he won the NFL rushing title. It was time for Little to pass the torch, and early in 1975, he announced he would do that following the season. Ironically, Armstrong suffered a severe hamstring tear in the fourth game at Pittsburgh and missed the remainder of the season. Little, along with fullback Jon Keyworth, again had to

carry the load. It had been a disappointing season. The Broncos stood at 5–7 with two games remaining. On December 14 Denver was playing its final home game against the Philadelphia Eagles. It was the last time Floyd would play in a Bronco uniform. Denver closed the season the next week in Miami, but Little sat it out. His last hurrah was in front of the home folks.

The love affair between Little and the Mile High City started in 1967 and continues today. Many contemporary Bronco fans never saw Floyd play, but they are aware of his days as a Bronco. On the annual Alumni Sunday, Little's introduction still ignites the crowd. He no longer makes his home in Denver, but the city and its people are in his heart. He is a successful automobile dealer in Seattle but sees as many Bronco games as he can.

Denver had never signed its number one draft pick until Little in 1967. The NFL-AFL merger brought on a common draft, and Coach Lou Saban chose the running back from Syracuse, who was the first three-time All-American since Doak Walker. Little would wear number 44 for the Broncos, the same number he wore for the Orangemen. This is significant because the Syracuse tradition is that only the very best running backs wear number 44. The legendary Jim Brown was the first to wear it, then Ernie Davis, and then Little. No one will ever wear it again in Denver. With John Elway's number 7 and Frank Tripucka's number 18, it's one of three numbers retired.

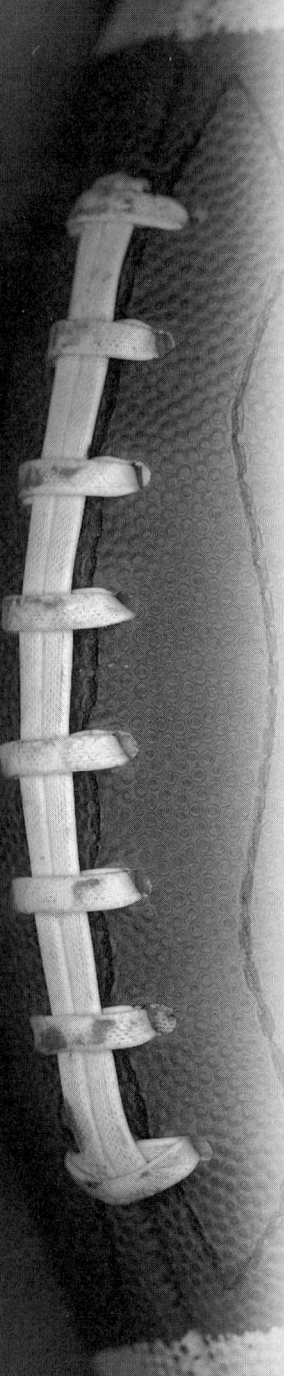

One Final Moment of Glory

Late in that Philadelphia game, the Broncos were leading but needed one more score to clinch it. With the ball at the Denver 34-yard line, Little wanted one final moment of glory. He asked quarterback Charley Johnson to call his number. Johnson chuckles about the situation, pointing out that everybody remembers that game as Floyd's last game, "but it was my last game too." Little was aware of that when he went to the huddle and asked Johnson to get him the ball. Little remembers, "I told Charley, this is our last time, let's do it right. Hit me with a screen pass and I'll complete the deal."

Did that really happen? Johnson says, "Floyd may have come in the huddle and said something, but I don't remember what. However, let me say that whatever he wanted to do, we did it."

Johnson hit Little with that screen pass into the right flat. He got by the line of scrimmage, aided by a good block from wide receiver Haven Moses. He got more help on the way as he weaved his way through Eagle defenders, broke into the clear, and headed toward the legendary South Stands. He didn't stop until he was in the end zone. Mile High Stadium was bedlam. Little recalls, "Haven got me a block at the line of scrimmage, then he passed me up and made another one downfield. I thought to myself, it is really time to quit when someone makes a block on the line then gets up and makes another one downfield and you're running all out."

Veteran quarterback Charley Johnson was talked into throwing Floyd Little that famous pass that went for a touchdown in Little's final game. Johnson retired after that season too. (Courtesy Rich Clarkson and Associates)

"I had several of the players from the Eagles come over during the game and congratulate me, not for just being a great player, but being a great person, one who helped perpetuate the game that they all loved. They said they were going to miss me. You know, we're playing, the game is still going, and there is this dialogue going on with the guys on the other side of the line. Several times I got tearful. By the end of the game I was an emotional wreck."

Little says the last two minutes were extremely difficult. "I looked up at the clock and it was the two-minute warning. I lost it. For some twenty years I'd been in competitive sports and as the clock clicked down, I was like, oh my God, I'm never going to play here again."

As the final second expired, the Broncos had a 25–10 victory, the players and fans lifted Little and carried him off the field to a standing ovation.

Little was not happy on draft day. He had always dreamed of playing for the New York Jets, but he now knew this was not possible. He had never been west of New York, until he and his wife, Joyce, visited Denver. Little says it was love at first sight. He made his home in Denver and became one of the city's leading citizens. His outgoing personality and charm added to the popularity he established on the football field. He never turned down a request from a charitable organization — no cause was too small. He gave his name and support to many civic projects. He was one of the key people on the organizing committee that bid successfully for the 1976 Winter Olympic Games for Denver. Unfortunately, a 1972 referendum cut off funding for the committee, and the games were lost. It was a bitter defeat for Little, who worked hard to solve many of the problems the committee faced.

Little's smile was infectious, but underneath that jovial exterior burned a great desire to achieve and to win. There was a private rage in Floyd Little. He explains: "I'd always been told as a youngster that I wasn't big enough [5'10", 195], strong enough, fast enough, or smart enough. I was always told, 'you can't.' It built up a lot of hostility in me. I wanted to prove to the world that I could not be judged by another's standards. I had to be judged by my own. That angered me more than anything else in the world, to be told that I couldn't do something. If you told me that, you had something to reckon with, because I knew I could. Even in college I felt that every time I stepped on the field, I had to prove myself."

It was no different in the professional ranks. Little started slowly, and again he found himself being questioned. Director of Player Personnel, later General Manager, Fred Gehrke said, "Little couldn't block, catch a pass, or protect himself when he got here."

Little carried something else into professional football—his bowlegs. He hated the bowlegs. "As a youngster, before I went to bed at night, I'd wrap my legs. I put belts around my thighs, my knees, and my calves. I was always hoping I'd wake up one day and my legs would be straight."

As his football career progressed, Little realized that the bowlegs were an asset. He had better balance because of his wide stance. "It allowed me to get away from defenders. I could do things that guys without the parenthesis between their legs couldn't do. A lot of times it takes both arms to tackle a runner. With the wide stance, defenders couldn't get both arms around my legs, thus I broke a lot of tackles. So I think the bowlegs really had a lot to do with my balance, my strength, and my running power."

In his rookie season Little averaged a mere 2.9 yards per carry and complained that he didn't run the ball enough to get into a rhythm. He carried 130 times for 381 yards, the offensive load being spread among five running backs. His longest run from scrimmage was 14 yards, and he scored only one touchdown. It was on special teams where he excelled, averaging 16.9 yards on 16 punt returns, returning one 72 yards for a touchdown. He had 35 kickoff returns for an average of 26.9 yards, including one 60 yarder. The Broncos won only three games and had to endure a nine-game losing streak after winning the opener. Little wasn't accustomed to losing, and he vowed he would become a leader who would make Denver a winner.

That first year made him more dedicated, and his hard work and discipline led to improvement in 1968. He touched the ball more often, getting 158 carries for 584 yards. He scored three touchdowns. He became more involved in the passing game, catching nineteen passes for 331 yards. He led the league in kickoff returns, with a 25-yard average, and returned punts for an average of 10.9 yards. He was the only player in the American Football League to be in the top ten of rushing, punt returns, and kickoff returns. While still not a winner, the Broncos improved.

Little's numbers could have been better, but he was plagued by injuries in those early years. In 1969 he gained 729 yards and averaged 5 yards per carry, but the Broncos still managed to win only five games in this final year of the American Football League. But then, it looked like 1970 would be the year. Denver started off with four wins in the first five games but hit a tailspin, winning only one more game the rest of the way. Little established himself as one of the top runners in the now fully merged NFL. He carried 209 times for 901 yards. Again, there were high hopes in 1971, but Denver still managed only four wins. Despite the team's lack of success, Little had his best season, running for 1,133 yards and winning the NFL rushing title. He also earned a spot in the Pro Bowl. He added another 255 yards to his total as the Broncos' third-best receiver.

The coach who brought Little to Denver, Lou Saban, resigned after nine games in 1971. Saban's resignation hit Little hard. Saban was a coach from the old school and demanded a lot from his players. That suited Little just fine. Not that the two always got along. Little might be the only player in NFL history to be fired on the sideline.

When Saban resigned, Floyd began to think it might be time for him to go too. Lou Sahadi, in his book *Broncos*, quotes him as saying, "In leaving, Saban just did something I've been thinking of doing. I think it's the type of people playing the game now. Every year they've got a different attitude. They don't understand what the game is and what it means. One

Floyd Little won the NFL rushing title in 1971, gaining 1,113 yards, and making him the first Broncos running back to gain more than 1,000 yards in a single season. (Courtesy Rich Clarkson and Associates)

Little Gets Fired during a Game

The Broncos appeared to be cruising to a victory over Buffalo by running out the clock. Floyd Little ran a sweep, lost the ball, and the Bills recovered. Little had to make a tackle to save a touchdown. Buffalo kicked a field goal to take the lead. As Little left the field, Coach Lou Saban was furious and yelled to Fred Gehrke, the player personnel director, that he wanted him out.

Little recalls, "Lou told me to get off the sideline, that I was finished, so I started walking to the locker room. The more I thought about it, the madder I got. I was around the 20 yard line on the south end and Denver had the ball on the north 20. I ran on the field yelling to Fran Lynch to get out of the game. As I passed the bench, Lou was screaming at me to get off the field and take a shower. Poor Fran, when I got to the huddle, Lou was yelling at Lynch to stay in the game and I was telling him to get out of there. Fran left. I pleaded my case with quarterback Marlin Briscoe. I told Briscoe to throw it as far as he could, that I would go get it."

Add another chapter in the legend of Floyd Little. He did catch the ball and it set up a game-winning field goal.

Saban got to the dressing room first. Little walked by him and apologized for his actions. Little remembers, "He said, 'you've got one more week,' then turned to a couple of reporters and said, 'He's beautiful.'" Later, Saban told him that Little had a job as long as Saban had a job.

game I had to almost kill a couple of guys at halftime for their attitude. You can't get them to do anything extra. I don't mind doing it. I want to. It's part of the game. I saw a couple of guys out there who could have done more. It's things like this that make you want to say the hell with it."

The positive-thinking John Ralston became the coach in 1972. After a successful career in the college ranks, Ralston brought a college atmosphere to the team. Ralston was a disciple of Dale Carnegie's "power of positive thinking." He admitted he had a lot of learning to do but set a goal of winning the Super Bowl. He said, "My basic philosophy is if you hang in there tough enough, long enough, work hard enough, dedicate yourself with a positive approach, anything can be accomplished." This meshed with Little's philosophy, and besides Ralston had gotten rid of some of the players who didn't buy into his requirements of hard work and dedication—the same group that had Little thinking of getting out of the game in 1971. Little's enthusiasm was renewed, and he developed a close relationship with Ralston, one that continues today.

Little couldn't help having a little fun with the always-focused Ralston. The new coach wanted to know more about his players and gave the team a series of psychological tests. Little recalls that Ralston called him into his office, saying, "I'm studying your test results and I'm really concerned about you. Your test results show that you are a homicidal maniac. You're the number one guy in the whole organization, we had no idea about this in your character."

Little asked, "What's a homicidal maniac?"

Ralston answered, "It's a guy who could just kill without any feeling."

Little shrugged and said, "Yeah, that's me. I'm a homicidal maniac okay."

At times Little's antics on the field made the test analysis seem fairly accurate. He never backed down from a confrontation, and at least once he carried it to an extreme. Little tells the story of the time he went out for a swing pass and while watching the ball was blindsided by a linebacker. Floyd recalls,

"He knocked me back 6 yards, busted my face mask, busted my nose, busted my mouth. He really coldcocked me. What really makes me mad is that I didn't get a chance to get back at him, because I was out for the rest of the game. I went after him after the game, but he took off to the locker room. Man, you think those linebackers can't run, but he outran me to the door. He stayed in there, so I stayed right by the door figuring he would have to come out sooner or later. There I was, still in my uniform, when one of our equipment people came over and said that we had to go, that the plane was waiting and that the coach said either you're going to get on the bus and go with us or you're going to stay here. I really was tempted to stay. I'd never been hit like that before in my life. I was so upset that I couldn't get him back. Here it is, years later, and I'm still talking about it."

In 1972, despite missing the last two games with an injury, he gained 859 yards and scored 9 touchdowns. He also caught 28 passes for 366 yards and 4 touchdowns. The Broncos still could not get above the five-win mark, but with Ralston's drafting skill, Denver was obviously a team on the rise.

Little was the workhorse in the 1973 season when Denver posted its first winning season in the fourteen-year history of the club. He carried the ball 256 times for 979 yards and 12 touchdowns. Little was most effective when running behind the effective blocking of fullback Joe Dawkins, but Ralston wanted to use his top draft choice, Armstrong, and began to experiment with what he called his "pony backfield." Both were relatively small backs and did give defenses problems. Ralston used the "pony" a lot more in 1974, but Little's production was cut to 312 yards and one touchdown. He carried 117 times as Armstrong became the featured back and won the NFL rushing title with 1,407 yards on 263 carries.

That brings us back to that misty night in 1975 when Little played his final game. At the time Little was the seventh leading rusher in NFL history. He had 6,323 career yards, a Bronco mark that stood until 1998, when Terrell Davis moved past him on his way to a 2,000-yard rushing season. Davis also passed Little in the total yards from scrimmage (rushing and receiving), most rushing touchdowns, and most total touchdowns. Little still holds the Bronco record for most combined yardage (rushing, receiving, and returns) with 12,157.

Little was one of the original four Broncos inducted into Denver's Ring of Fame and is a member of the Colorado Sports Hall of Fame. One honor that he richly deserves, that has eluded him, is membership in the Pro Football Hall of Fame. The fact that he labored mostly on a poor team that didn't get a great deal of national exposure has hurt his chances. There is still a chance through the Old-Timers Committee.

Floyd Little truly earned the name, *Mr. Bronco.*

Make Those Miracles Happen

"The miracle has happened. . . . The Broncos are going to the Super Bowl."

Those were words of my partner, Bob Martin, on January 1, 1978, as the final seconds had ticked off the clock with the Oakland Raiders standing helpless on the sidelines. The Denver Broncos touched off a celebration on the field that would carry on into the night in the State of Colorado, and indeed in the entire Rocky Mountain region.

The Broncos had beaten the Raiders 20–17 to win the American Football Conference championship. It was only the fourth winning season in franchise history and it did seem like a miracle that Denver was headed to the New Orleans Superdome.

When Broncos fans awoke with a gigantic hangover on January 2, they picked up the *Denver Post* and read these words penned by Hall of Fame columnist Dick Connor:

> The first thing we're going to have to do is get the language straight.
> Carefully now, like the first sip of wine, try it.
> Super Bowl.
> Fine. Now gulp. There's more. All you want. For

the next two weeks, that's all you'll hear or read or see, and maybe near Jan. 14 you'll be gagging on it. By Jan. 14 you'll be hung over on the stuff.

But now, it's time to savor, and enjoy, and let yourself get a little giddy. Eighteen years on the temperance wagon are long enough. Pour it down.

The Denver Broncos, the clown princes of the old AFL, the court jesters, have seized control of the kingdom and toppled the king himself.

This is a book of stories. This story is of a team, a city, a state, and a region, which in a five-month period tasted things that had been only in their dreams.

Under John Ralston the Broncos became a winner. Their first winning record was 1973, followed by another in 1974, and the best record in team history at 9–5 in 1976. Yet a playoff berth still eluded them. The ever-optimistic Ralston looked forward to 1977, but he didn't make it to the season.

Ralston came to Denver with great credentials. On the strong arm of Jim Plunkett, his Stanford teams had scored two straight upsets in the Rose Bowl, over Ohio State and Michigan.

Ralston was a student of Dale Carnegie and was a disciple of his "power of positive thinking." Ralston's cheerful and effervescent attitude was infectious. He was a fun guy to be around, but many of his veteran players didn't agree. They didn't like the rah-rah attitude and felt they had left that behind in college. There was a tough side of Ralston and he got rid of the players who didn't buy into his program.

One of Ralston's innovations during training camp and the season was the 10:00 P.M. "Ice Cream Social." It was mandatory for players to attend. It was also a way to make sure

John Ralston took over the Broncos in 1972 after successive Rose Bowl victories at Stanford. He brought Denver its first winning season in 1973. (Courtesy Rich Clarkson and Associates)

they were all about ready to be tucked in. Moving the training camp to Pomona, California, was not a popular move. The Cal Poly campus was isolated and it was extremely hot in July and August. Brush fires on the hills surrounding the practice field were not unusual and many were the afternoons that the players had to contend with the smoke as well as the heat.

Fun and Games with Uncle John

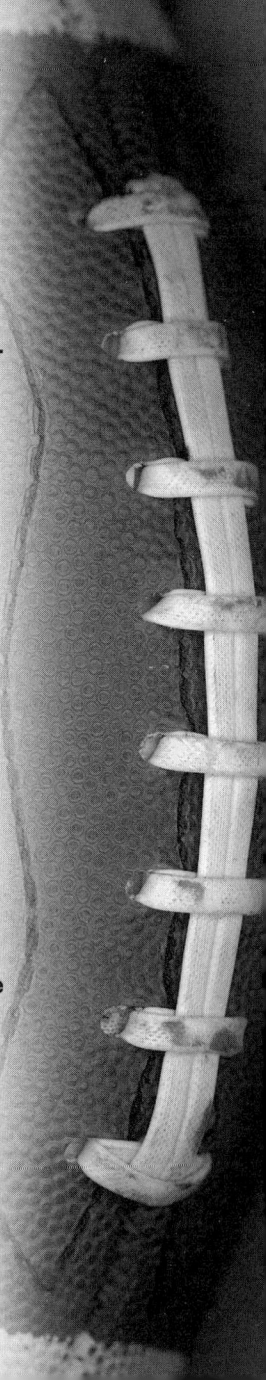

The players had their fun with Ralston. One day, he came bounding into a meeting and wrote the word ball on the blackboard. He enthused, "The word ball is always associated with a game. Racquetball . . . baseball . . . basketball . . . football." As he continued, a voice from the back of the room said, "Meatball." The players cracked up.

Another time, Ralston started the meeting with a big rubber band. He stretched it and said it was indicative of the defense. It would stretch, but not break. When it popped, they were rolling in the aisles.

Perhaps the best story of the Ralston era is one for which you must have faith that it really happened. Ralston loved to join the team on the field just prior to the kickoff. He would be jumping around and trying to "fire them up." Before one game, in a particularly enthusiastic moment, he exclaimed, "My biggest disappointment is that I can't play in this game. If I had a helmet, I would." Fran Lynch took off his helmet, handed it to Ralston, and headed to the sideline. They finally got the laughter under control so they could line up for the kickoff.

Ralston loves football and is still involved in the game today, working with the National Football Foundation, the College Football Hall of Fame, and San Jose State University. After being fired in Denver, he never got another head coaching job in the NFL, but he did in the USFL, and then returned to college coaching at San Jose.

He's still the same cheerful, optimistic guy that I first met more than thirty years ago.

Ralston's departure from the Broncos was unexpected. Owner Gerald Phipps felt the dual jobs of coach and general manager were too much and made Director of Player Personnel Fred Gehrke the general manager. Ralston seemed to adjust to this, but twelve veteran players led a revolt against their coach. It was an ugly time, and on January 31, 1977, Ralston announced his resignation, but it was no secret he was fired. Robert "Red" Miller, who had been an assistant in Denver during the 1960s, was hired the next day. Miller was a quality offensive line coach and had a good reputation as an offensive coordinator.

A key move for the Broncos was the acquisition of Craig Morton, the veteran quarterback, from the Giants. He had quarterbacked Dallas in a Super Bowl and became an instant leader in Denver.

Joe Collier stayed as defensive coordinator. Under Saban and Ralston, he crafted the 3–4 alignment that would become known as the "Orange Crush."

After Denver opened with four straight wins, first place in the Western Division was at stake in game five in Oakland. The Raiders were the defending world champions and riding a seventeen-game winning streak. The game produced one of football's more memorable plays. Leading 14–7, the Broncos were at the Raider 25. Jim Turner trotted out to try a 33-yard field goal. Quarterback Norris Weese was the holder, and when he took the snap, he jumped up and let the pressure come. Turner ambled out to the side and turned down field. The Raiders realized it was a fake and turned their attention to the receivers. Turner went unnoticed. In his ancient high-top shoes, he was plodding downfield 10 yards behind everybody. Weese launched the pass. The only question now was, "Would Turner catch it?" He did and lumbered into the end zone and into history.

Denver was up 30–7 when Tom Jackson, never the timid soul, recovered a fumble in front of the Raiders bench, waved the ball in front of Coach John Madden, and screamed his most famous quote, "It's all over, fat man."

After Denver went 6–0 at Cincinnati, they lost their first game of the season in a rematch with the Raiders. They started the second half of the season with a solid win over Pittsburgh and then pulled out road wins at San Diego and Kansas City. The "M and M Connection" (Morton to Haven Moses) produced come-from-behind wins in both games.

The Broncos were 9–1 and heading home from Kansas City for a showdown with the Eastern Division leading Baltimore Colts, also 9–1. After the Raiders lost to the Chargers, Denver was alone at the top of the West.

Confidence was building in the Bronco locker room. They had survived two straight close calls on the road and controlled their own destiny in the Western Division race. The Orange Crush was reminded that it would have to rule the day against the formidable Colt offense, led by quarterback Bert Jones and running back Lydell Mitchell.

Tom Jackson broke open a close game with a fourth-quarter interception that he returned 73 yards for a touchdown, the longest interception return in team history. The Broncos won 27–13.

Denver was 10–1, the best record in the NFL, but the word *playoffs* was forbidden in the Bronco camp.

Denver won in Houston, 24–14, and as the team boarded buses for the airport, the Raiders–Rams game was underway on the West Coast. The charter airplane was somewhere over the Texas panhandle when the pilot asked Miller to come to the cockpit. He told Red that the Rams had just beaten the Raiders, and the Broncos were the champions of the Western Division.

The Orange Crush

Joe Collier had no idea that his defense would go down in history. He changed his scheme out of necessity.

"We were a four-man line team," Collier said, "then one year we lost Lyle Alzado on the first play of the first game with a knee injury, so we decided to switch over to the 3–4. We had more good linebackers than we had linemen. We had been playing the 3–4 a little bit, but now we went to it fulltime. We put in more variations and the players played it for a while. You could just see it coming together. The key was that we kept that group together. You know, some of those guys were eight, nine, or ten years together. That was one of the big factors. We didn't lose guys through free agency in those days. Consequently, when you get the same guys playing together in one particular system, you have success. And the defense evolved. It just came on like gangbusters."

One key to 3–4 is the linebackers. Denver had Randy Gradishar, Tom Jackson, Bob Swenson, and Joe Rizzo. Collier said, "They were a great group of guys. They were all leaders. Another key is to have unselfish linemen. They aren't the kingpins of the defense. We had Rubin Carter, Alzado, and Barney Chavous who took a lot of the punishment, because they have to turn things to the linebackers. So it was not only the linebackers, it was the front seven."

The secondary gave support too, led by the captain, Billy Thompson. Collier said, "Billy was a great strong safety. He was the best run defender that we had. . . . He was the oldest guy and a great leader. Steve

Linebacker Randy Gradishar (53) huddles with the Orange Crush.
(Courtesy Rich Clarkson and Associates)

Foley was a quarterback in college and became a fine free safety. . . .
Louis Wright was in a league by himself as a cornerback. . . . If there
was a great receiver on the team we were playing, we would say, 'Louie
you cover this guy and the rest of us will play defense.' We added
Bernard Jackson in 1977 and he was the final cog that we needed."

Red announced the final score on the airplane's public-address system. I'm sure that the residents of Dumas and Dalhart, Texas, 32,000 feet below, heard the roar. The Broncos were heading to the playoffs with the home field advantage throughout.

The party was on. You had to be part of that celebration to truly appreciate it. The airplane was bedlam. There were shouts and screams, there were tears, there were hugs, and then there was secretly hidden champagne. It was a chore for the flight crew to get everybody to fasten seat belts for the landing.

The party on the ground was getting revved up as well. The throng greeting the team at the airport was as fired up as the guys in the air. There were more than a few folks late for work that Monday morning.

The Broncos finished out the season with a win over San Diego and a loss in Dallas. The final record was 12–2.

Going into the playoffs, Miller had a major concern. His quarterback was hurt. The pounding Morton took through the season had caught up with the "old man." His right hip was a massive bruise. Morton had desperately wanted to play against his old team, the Cowboys. Miller knew the prudent thing to do was to rest him, but he agreed to start him. It was evident that Morton was hurting and after the first series went to the bench.

The week before Christmas 1977 was like no other in the history of the Queen City of the Plains. Santa Claus took a back seat to the Denver Broncos. One Santa even appeared in an orange suit. Many toted home orange Christmas trees. Orange cars appeared on the streets. The most popular and most played song in Denver was not "Silent Night," but Jon Keyworth's "Make Those Miracles Happen." The Bronco fullback would later recall that he was sitting in a bar with some friends and decided to do a song that turned out to be a mix of late 1970 disco and Barry Manilow. Two friends collaborated with Jon to write the song.

Although he would never be mistaken for Elvis, Keyworth could turn a tune, and on occasion he appeared at clubs around town. In two weeks, 50,000 45 rpm records were pressed and record stores couldn't keep them in stock. Keyworth sang "Miracles" on the *Dinah Shore Show*. Jon said, "That was fun."

The nation's football fans still didn't believe. The Steelers were favored in the divisional playoff game. Wide receiver Jack Dolbin later said, "Nobody took us seriously. People east of the Mississippi River had no idea what kind of football team we were."

Christmas Eve finally arrived, sunny with temperatures in the forties. If there were sugarplums dancing in the heads of the 75,000 who jammed Mile High Stadium, they were colored orange. The unlucky folks without tickets were crowded in front of television sets. Santa could wait.

The playoff-hardened Steelers had other ideas and entered Mile High Stadium with a swagger. It was the Orange Crush against the Steel Curtain. The game that followed was a Yuletide gift to the nation's football fans. There were ties at 7, 14, and 21. Tom Jackson again made big plays, picking off two Terry Bradshaw passes. Late in the game, when a deep pass from Morton settled into Dolbin's arms in the end zone, the issue was decided. The earth along I–25 in northwest Denver was vibrating like an earthquake from the noise. Denver was headed to the AFC Championship Game, against none other than the defending champion Oakland Raiders. Merry Christmas!

"If You'll Tie My Shoes, I'll Play"

Craig Morton's bruised body got worse as the season wore on. The Morton drama played out behind closed doors during that holiday week. The scenario could not happen today. Craig struggled to get out of bed on Christmas morning. Not wanting to disturb anyone's holiday, he gutted it out until the following morning, when he went to the training room. The bruise on the hip and buttocks was massive and ugly. Morton went to the hospital, but Red Miller didn't want the Raiders to know about it. Somehow he convinced the hospital staff to stay buttoned up. If anybody did talk, it wasn't reported in the media. The players also kept their mouths zipped and prayed for Morton's recovery. He was released Friday afternoon, less than forty-eight hours before the game. While the fans celebrated New Year's Eve, Morton rested.

The tailgating was well underway in the parking lot, and Bronco "Watch Parties" started all over town, as the drama was playing out under the South Stands. Morton later related, "Everyone in the locker room was watching me, so I broke the ice. I told them, I would play if they didn't let the Raiders hit me." It was a brave front, but after he struggled into his uniform, he couldn't bend over to tie his shoes. Morton called Miller over and told him, "If you'll tie my shoes, I'll play."

Red Miller will never forget tying those shoelaces, and Morton will never forget what happened over the next four hours.

The year 1978 started with a crystal-clear Colorado morning with temperatures in the teens. It would be an ideal day. These two teams knew each other well. Miller wanted to protect Morton and had a run-oriented game plan. Morton gave Denver an early lead on an uncharacteristic and bold 74-yard pass to Moses that caught the Raiders by surprise. The "M and M Connection" had done it again.

At the half it was still 7–3. Players related that Miller didn't say a thing. He simply wrote on the blackboard, "Thirty Minutes to the Super Bowl."

Both teams blew scoring opportunities in the tense third quarter. Miller was watching Morton closely as were the Raiders. He was walking with an obvious limp. Denver got a break on a play at the Raider 2 yard line, when after a fumble by Rob Lytle, the officials ruled the whistle had blown *before* the fumble. Given a second chance, Morton called a play that, considering his condition, wouldn't be easy to execute. He rolled out and pitched the ball to Keyworth, who walked into the end zone against the mad and fooled Raiders. Denver had a 14–3 lead. The Crush had played a lot and was wearing down. It was soon 14–10, with fourteen minutes still to play.

The tension mounted as the game went on. It was almost unbearable when Denver faced a third and 5 at the Oakland 12 with less than eight minutes remaining. Morton wanted a touchdown, but he didn't want to make a mistake that would cost a chance at a field goal. The play was a pass to Riley Odoms, but when the big tight end was double covered, he looked elsewhere. He was about to dump the ball when he saw number 25 break from the outside toward the middle of the end zone running along the end line. Morton fired. Moses went high in the air and caught the ball but had to get down with his feet in bounds. He hung in the air for what seemed like an eternity. When he finally fell to the turf, the officials checked his feet and threw up their hands. It was a touchdown. "Rocky Mountain Thunder" was never louder. In their excitement the Broncos misplayed the extra point attempt, and the ten-point lead kept the Raiders in the hunt. Stabler moved the Raiders for 74 yards and 7 points in just 8 plays; 3:16 remained. The margin was three points.

Quarterback Craig Morton (7) performed courageously in leading the Broncos over the Oakland Raiders, 20–17, in the AFC Championship Game on January 1, 1978. (Courtesy Rich Clarkson and Associates)

After the kickoff the ball was at the Bronco 17, and the Broncos were three minutes away from the Super Bowl. Morton told the team he was going to keep it on the ground and that two first downs would win it.

Denver had one first down by the two-minute warning. Oakland used its final time out as the Broncos faced third and 3. Morton reminded the team that they were 3 yards away from New Orleans. This time he put his trust in Otis Armstrong, who had won the NFL rushing title a few years earlier. On that play he gained the most important 4 yards of his career. Denver had a first down and all the Raiders could do was watch the clock run down.

I was on the air from the locker room and remember Morton, with tears streaming down his face, struggling back to the doorway so he could watch the goal posts come down. Morton had completed 10 of 20 passes for 224 yards and 2 touchdowns, and he hadn't practiced a down all week. It was one of the most courageous performances in Bronco history.

All of the trappings that surround today's Super Bowls hadn't yet been invented. The team hotels were near the New Orleans International Airport, less than luxurious. The Cowboys were at the sprawling Hilton complex and the Broncos about a mile away at the Sheraton. The biggest story on the first night was Armstrong's sprint down to the lobby, in horror, after finding a huge Louisiana cockroach in his bed. The players complained that paint was peeling off the walls and that the food was terrible. The McDonald's down the street got a lot of business. Then there was the time the elevator broke down with several players inside. In his book, *Blitz*, Tom Jackson wrote, "We were beginning to think we might not even make it to the game. The headline would read, '32 Broncos Eaten by Roaches, Rest Lost in Elevator.'"

The players were dismayed by the practice facility, abandoned and rusting Tulane Stadium. It was a bus ride across the city. The Cowboys were at the plush New Orleans Saints facility in Metairie, a stone's throw from their hotel.

Usually the weather in New Orleans is tropical, but this January it was cloudy, cold, windy, and damp. The players shivered through their practice sessions. Keyworth shivered for another reason. He received a death threat and security was tightened. It was yet another distraction.

Meanwhile, Bronco fans were painting Bourbon Street orange. The game captured the imagination of the nation and ninety million would watch on television. It was the largest audience to watch a sporting event. Some of the players came out for early warm-ups wearing replicas of the detested vertically striped socks to show their pride in the history of the franchise.

The Cowboys greeted Morton with a fierce pass rush and kept him on the run all day. The Doomsday Defense picked off four of Morton's passes and recovered four fumbles. This was not the way to win a Super Bowl. Despite the mistakes, with twelve minutes to play in the third quarter, Denver was down by only ten points, 13–3. Was another miracle possible for this team?

Dallas made it 20–3, but Upchurch returned the kickoff 67 yards to the Cowboy 26. Miller replaced the struggling Morton with the more mobile Norris Weese. The youngster led them to a touchdown in less than a minute. It was 20–10 with still five minutes to go in the third quarter. The fans were thinking about miracles again. But there were none left. Dallas won it 27–10.

Despite the disappointment, the Denver fans were wonderful. As the team left the field on the verge of tears, the fans were on their feet screaming, "We love you, Broncos." The city had a huge celebration when the team returned.

More exciting times were ahead for Bronco fans, but the Miracle Team of 1977 will never be forgotten.

"We Got These Guys Right Where We Want 'Em"

W e got these guys right where we want 'em." That arguably is the most famous line ever uttered in a Denver Broncos huddle.

The place was the AFC Championship Game following the 1986 season—played on January 11, 1987. It was Denver's first chance to make it back to the Super Bowl since 1977, but the Browns playing at home in Cleveland Stadium, in terrible weather conditions and supported by rabid fans, were favored and had just taken a 20–13 lead with 5:43 to go in the game. To make matters worse the ensuing kickoff was misplayed and rolled to the Bronco 2 yard line where Broncos special teams player Gene Lang fell on it.

Denver was 98 yards away, needing a touchdown to tie the game. Could the heralded but controversial number one draft choice from 1983, John Elway, take his team to victory?

That question was also on the minds of the offensive team as they went to the huddle in their own end zone. Guard Keith Bishop broke the trance by saying, "We got these guys right where we want 'em."

It went down in the annals of football as "The Drive." We

will take a closer look at The Drive, but first the story of how the Broncos came to that moment and became the AFC's dominant team in the late 1980s.

Even though it was a stable franchise, the Broncos would change hands twice in the early part of the decade. In 1981, with rumors of a strike in 1982, and the illness of owner Gerry Phipps's wife, Gerry and Allan Phipps decided to sell. Edgar Kaiser Jr., grandson of one of the twentieth century's business giants, Henry J. Kaiser, purchased the team. His home was in Canada, but he had oil interests in Colorado. Three years later, he would sell to another Canadian businessman, Pat Bowlen.

Kaiser made changes at the outset, firing General Manager Fred Gehrke and Coach Red Miller. Kaiser had everything in place before going public. He hired Minnesota Vikings administrator Grady Alderman to be the general manager. Kaiser targeted Dallas assistant coach Dan Reeves as his head coaching choice. Kaiser, his business advisor, Hein Poulus, and Alderman were the only ones present for the interview with Reeves, who arrived at one of Kaiser's Canadian homes on a float plane. There were no negotiations. Kaiser simply offered Reeves the job. A day later, as Reeves was flying from Dallas to Denver, to be announced as the new coach, Kaiser fired Gehrke and Miller.

Red Miller deserved a better fate. At least he deserved a decent "firing," rather than the way it happened. The ownership has every right to make changes in the direction it wants to take a football team, or any business. Some close to the situation say Red might have come on a little strong to Kaiser about control of the football operation. The way in which he found out that he was fired had to be difficult for a man who had taken his team to the Super Bowl just four years before.

While Reeves was on his way to Denver, it was a normal off-season workday for Miller and his staff. Defensive line coach Stan Jones was in the weight room supervising the off-season training program when secondary coach Richie McCabe walked in all excited. He said he just heard from friends on the Minnesota Vikings staff that the ownership had hired a new coach and that Red had been fired (apparently the word leaked out of Minnesota, because it was the organization that Grady Alderman was leaving to become the Broncos general manager).

Jones said, "That's ridiculous. Red's upstairs meeting with the offensive staff."

McCabe stood by his story, and Jones asked him, "Don't you think you ought to say something to Red about this?"

McCabe agreed, so the two went upstairs. Richie said, "Red, I just heard that you got fired."

A shocked Miller answered, "We'll see about that."

Jones said, "He got on the phone, rings up Kaiser, had a short conversation, put the phone down and said, 'Yep, you're right, I got fired.' That's how he found out about it."

Miller was deeply hurt by the firing but remained a gentleman. He didn't want to do anything to hurt the team and obviously had no personal animosity toward Reeves.

The quick settlement of the Reeves deal by a handshake left a lot of things unresolved. Predictable problems on the division of power and the owner's involvement quickly surfaced. Kaiser didn't like the team's financial situation, particularly with regard to player salaries, reportedly the highest in the NFL. He wanted to trade All-Pro linebacker Randy Gradishar because he made too much money. Reeves enlisted defensive coordinator Joe Collier's help to convince Kaiser that he couldn't trade a keystone of the defense just

Canadian millionaire Edgar Kaiser (left) purchased the Broncos in 1981 and named Dan Reeves (right) the head coach. Kaiser was one year older than Reeves. (Courtesy Rod Hanna/Rich Clarkson and Associates)

because of his salary. Kaiser gave them a lecture on the economics of business and suggested that Randy take a salary cut. Collier told Kaiser that was out of the question. Reeves and Collier feel the only reason that Kaiser relented was because they convinced him that the fans and media would be in an uproar if he traded one of the team's most popular players.

Kaiser did engineer the deal that brought John Elway to Denver. Elway was adamant that he would not play in

Baltimore, but the Colts drafted him as the first player in the 1983 draft. The question was, "Would Elway agree to play for the Broncos?"

Kaiser wanted a quick answer so there could be no backing out of the deal. He had his private jet pick up Elway's agent, Marvin Demoff, and fly him to Denver. It was past 8:00 P.M. when Reeves, Demoff, and Kaiser met at a private air terminal while another of Kaiser's jets was flying Elway to the rendezvous. Demoff got on the airplane with John, and when he emerged, Elway was a Bronco. By now it was close to ten o'clock. Kaiser and Reeves didn't want to sit on it. They called a press conference, which took place shortly before midnight.

Elway's reputation as the "Comeback Kid" was building by 1986. The biggest was yet to come—the AFC Championship Game in Cleveland. Denver had never won a postseason game away from home. This one didn't appear to be easy. The Browns had everything going. They had had a great year and the fans were rabid. The most rabid occupied the "Dawg Pound" on the lake end of antiquated Cleveland Stadium.

On this day there were nearly 80,000 screaming "Dawgs" all over the stadium as the game began. Elway and Bernie Kosar sparred with each other through the first half, which ended in a 10–10 tie. Rich Karlis gave Denver a 13–10 lead in the third quarter with a 26-yard field goal. Cleveland got the three points back early in the fourth period and then went ahead on a 48-yard pass play from Kosar to Brian Brennan; 5:43 remained in the game. Then came the misplayed kickoff and Denver had the ball 98 yards away from tying the game, having to drive toward the lake and into the frigid wind.

The players in the huddle in the end zone said John Elway looked fierce. It was like he was in a trance.

The Broncos moved away from their own goal line, got a first down, and on second and 7 at the 15, Elway ran for 11 yards to the 26.

"They came with a rush. I looked up field. They were soft, so I took off."

Then he hit Steve Sewell for a 22-yard gain to the 48.

"The time wasn't a factor at that point. We still had time to run. I came back with a play action fake and passed to Sewell. With each successful play we gained more confidence."

A 12-yard pass to Steve Watson put the ball on the Cleveland 40, but then Elway was sacked for a loss of 8 yards.

"I took a time out after that. The last thing you want there is a sack. Give them some credit, they were really playing hard."

The Broncos were moving ever closer to the "Dawg Pound." The crowd was loud and as usual they were pelting the field with dog bones and other items. The next play was almost a disaster for Denver.

"The crowd was so loud that we had gone to a silent cadence, trying to time it with the motion. I was in the shotgun and Watson was in motion. The snap was a little early and it hit Watson in the hip. I was fortunate enough to be able to get the ball and hit Mark [Jackson] and get a first down.

"The 20-yard gain put the ball at the Cleveland 28. First down. A pass to Steve Sewell covered 14 yards and the ball was at the Browns' 14 yard line with fifty-seven-seconds to go. The Cleveland players hooked their thumbs in their belts. They were tired and worried."

Oddly, the crowd grew quiet.

After an incompletion, Elway ran 9 yards to the Cleveland 5. It was third and 1.

Cleveland Had Gone to the Dogs

The city on the shores of Lake Erie had gone to the dogs. Picking up the cue from the fans in the "Dawg Pound," all Browns fans called themselves "Dawgs." When the Broncos arrived at the hotel on Friday evening, the street was jammed with fans, all barking, many wearing dog masks. My broadcast partner, Bob Martin, *Denver Post* columnist Dick Connor, and I went to Severance Hall for a concert given by the Cleveland Orchestra on Saturday night and when the last notes of the Sibelius Seventh Symphony were played, the audience burst into applause. The orchestra started barking at them. The audience got the idea and started barking too. I'm sure it was the rowdiest scene ever in the historic concert hall.

The weather was typical January in Cleveland. Cold, dreary, and on the night we arrived, it featured a few flurries. Because the team arrived late, the entire traveling party was invited to a special dinner at the hotel.

It was quite a spread, but what was weird was the music selected for the dinner—a young lady playing the harp. This is a football team, after all. She was playing a classical repertoire and Reeves was entranced. He moved his chair near her in the corner and asked if she could play country-western. She did and stayed well beyond her appointed time, with Reeves making request after request.

Outside, despite the weather, the barking continued, and through that night and Saturday night, cars circled the hotel blowing their horns. Anything to disrupt the visitors.

Cleveland Stadium was within walking distance of the hotel. The wind coming off the lake was stiff and cold. There was a freezing rain and the field was a quagmire. The Broncos dumped plans for a light workout and simply walked the sidelines.

It got colder overnight, and when the teams went out for the pregame warm-ups, the field was frozen solid. The skies were dark gray and the temperature was officially thirty degrees, but the fourteen-mile-per-hour wind off Lake Erie produced a wind chill of minus five.

If you have visions of a luxurious broadcast booth, think again. We climbed a ladder, went through a hole in the stadium roof, and walked across the roof to a wooden structure housing three broadcast booths separated by plain wooden walls. There was no way to shut out the cold wind. Our producer, Jerry Peters, had purchased two electric space heaters to give us some warmth.

Thankfully Cleveland Stadium, "The Mistake by the Lake," is gone now and the Browns have a brand new home.

Mark Jackson (80) celebrates in the Cleveland end zone after catching a 5-yard pass from John Elway, completing the famous 98-yard drive to tie the AFC Championship Game in the final seconds on January 11, 1987. (Courtesy Eric Lars Bakke)

"We had options on the next play. I had Mark [Jackson] coming in on a slant route. I saw the corner come off Mark; I saw a seam and threw a low heater. If Mark didn't get it, no one else would get it. All I could think of was get that ball to him. I don't remember ever throwing a ball as hard as I threw that ball."

Jackson went to his knees in the end zone and the ball was there. It settled into his arms and Denver was one point away from tying the game. Karlis had to kick on the open end, the worst side for a kicker. He scraped away the dog bones and booted it through.

Cleveland got the ball first in overtime, but now the Broncos had momentum. The Browns went 1–2–3–punt. Elway completed passes to Watson and Orson Mobley and had the ball in field-goal range. On three plays they moved it 7 yards closer, to the 15. The barefooted kicker, Karlis, pulled it to the left, but it was inside the upright and the Broncos won 23–20.

"That was the game that really got me started, where I could fulfill some of the expectations of me when I came into the league."

The Drive is a moment in sports that will never be forgotten.

An already long day became longer. The frustrated Cleveland fans reacted stupidly by calling in bomb threats to the team's chartered plane while the Broncos team bus made its way to Cleveland's Hopkins International Airport. Unknowingly, the team happily climbed aboard the charter. The decision was made to unload the aircraft and check all the baggage, team equipment, and the carry-on bags as well. It was nearing midnight when the weary, but happy, Broncos touched down at Stapleton. As the airplane taxied to the

United Airlines hangar on the perimeter of the airport, the occupants got their first glimpse of the crowd, estimated at between 10,000 and 20,000. An impromptu stage was set up on a hydraulic lift. Elway, Reeves, Bowlen, and some other players joined Governor Roy Romer and Mayor Federico Peña, while the rest of the plane's occupants made their way out of the mass of humanity. The crowds were lined along the road from the airport for more than a mile. Broncomania was alive and well. Before the Broncos departed for Pasadena for the Super Bowl, 63,000 attended a pep rally at Mile High Stadium.

The hottest team in football was the NFC champions, the New York Giants. They hadn't lost since October, winning eleven straight, including a 19–16 victory over the Broncos at the Meadowlands late in November. It had been an evenly matched game that New York won on an unlikely interception.

More than 101,000 were on hand at the Rose Bowl in Pasadena on a sunny, seventy-six-degree day, and when it was over they departed to the strains of "New York, New York." The Giants won 39–20.

There was another strike after the second game of the 1987 season. The owners followed through on their threat and hired replacement players. Denver replacements, with help from several players who crossed the picket line, went 2–1, instrumental in the team's drive for a second straight Super Bowl.

By the end of the season, they were on a roll. The Broncos were matched against Cleveland again in the AFC Championship Game and won 38–33. It appeared that the Browns might get a last second win this time as Earnest Byner headed for the Denver goal line in the final minute. On the 3 yard line, Jeremiah Castille stripped the ball and fell on the fumble to insure the Broncos victory.

Even though the Broncos jumped out with a 10–0 lead against the Washington Redskins in Super Bowl XXII, forty-two unanswered points later the final score was 42–10. Denver returned home a Super Bowl loser once again.

In 1989, for the third time in four years, the Broncos and Cleveland Browns met for the AFC championship and the outcome was the same. This time there was no need for final minute heroics as the Broncos won 37–21.

Denver fans had been burned three times in the Super Bowl and were wary of this one. In a classic battle between two of the top quarterbacks, Joe Montana and Elway, Montana stole the headlines. He completed 22 of 29 for 297 yards and 5 touchdowns, while Elway managed only 10 completions for 108 yards and no touchdowns. It was another Super humiliation for Denver, the game going to the 49ers 55–10. It was the worst defeat in Super Bowl history. The *Rocky Mountain News* headline read, "Nightmare."

The Broncos, with three Super Bowl appearances in four years, certainly were the dominant team in the AFC, but nationally they came off as losers. The citizens of Colorado, who identify so closely with the team, took it personal. There was no parade this time.

The Broncos Finally Win It All

T his one's for John," proclaimed owner Pat Bowlen when he hoisted the Lombardi Trophy in the postgame celebration of Super Bowl XXXII in San Diego. His Broncos had beaten the Green Bay Packers 31–24. Bowlen's sentiments were warranted. It had been a long road, but John Elway had finally arrived at the pinnacle of professional football. It was a huge victory for Denver fans, fearing a fifth Super Bowl loss.

An estimated 650,000 fans gathered along 17th Street for the eighteen-block parade, then converged on the Civic Center as the champion Broncos were welcomed home.

It took a while for the Broncos to get back to the Super Bowl after the humiliating 55–10 loss to the 49ers in January 1990. In 1991 they got back to the AFC Championship Game but fell to heavily favored Buffalo, 10–7.

The Bills were on a roll. The previous year, Buffalo clobbered the Raiders 51–3 in the championship game, before losing to the Giants in the Super Bowl 20–19 on a missed field goal in the final seconds. Buffalo made it four straight division championships in 1991 and was shooting for a second straight Super Bowl appearance.

It was an unusually balmy forty-two degrees in Buffalo that January 12. Rich Stadium was jammed; 80,272 fans were ready to cheer on the heavily favored Bills.

The Denver defense was superb against Jim Kelly and company and played well enough for Denver to win. Elway had to leave the game in the third quarter with a pulled thigh muscle and long-time backup quarterback Gary Kubiak almost pulled it out. With the Broncos down 10–0, Kubiak fashioned an 85-yard, 8-play drive, scoring on a 3-yard draw play. Denver was down by three with 1:43 to play.

After a successful onside kick, Denver had the ball at its own 49 with plenty of time and two timeouts. On first down Kubiak passed to Steve Sewell who picked up 7 yards, but fumbled at the end of the play. The Bills recovered and ran out the clock. Turnovers, three missed field goals, and other mistakes cost Denver a shot at a fifth Super Bowl, the fourth in six years.

It was Kubiak's final game. He announced his retirement and returned to his alma mater, Texas A&M, to begin his coaching career. Kubiak had worked under Mike Shanahan as a player and after two years at Texas A&M, he was called by Shanahan to join him in San Francisco, where Mike was offensive coordinator. The 49ers won the Super Bowl in 1994. When Shanahan was named head coach at Denver, he hired Kubiak as the offensive coordinator. Under Kubiak, the Broncos twice have been the NFL's number one offense.

Shanahan could have been the head coach in 1993 after Dan Reeves was fired, but Mike was reluctant to follow Reeves. Shanahan was quoted as saying, "Things had gotten bad between Dan and me and many thought I was after his job. I didn't want to be thought of as the guy who took Dan's job."

Bowlen next turned to Denver's defensive coordinator Wade Phillips. Bowlen felt that Reeves had too much control; Phillips went the other way, concentrating on coaching and letting others make the front office decisions. General

Gary Kubiak (left) was John Elway's backup and spent a lot of time next to Dan Reeves (right) on the sidelines, signaling the plays. (Courtesy Eric Lars Bakke/Rich Clarkson and Associates)

Manager John Beake gained more control of the football operation, negotiated contracts, and made many player decisions, aided by Bob Ferguson, the talented player personnel director. The NFL now had free agency, and Beake and Ferguson were able to strengthen the offensive line by signing Vikings lineman Brian Habib and Pro Bowler Gary Zimmerman. Elway finally had the offensive line he had longed for. The road to the world championship had begun.

Jim Fassel, who went on to coach the Giants, became offensive coordinator. He had been the offensive coordinator when Elway played at Stanford. Fassel ran the "West Coast"

Kubes to the Rescue

Gary Kubiak backed up John Elway for nine years. The two were roommates and the best of friends with the longest traveling gin rummy game in sports history. Kubiak played in 119 games for Denver and five times started for Elway, producing a 4–1 record.

In 1989 Denver was 8–2 and making a push to another Super Bowl when they faced an important game against the Redskins in Washington on Monday Night Football. Elway joined some of the Bronco brass for breakfast at the White House with President George H. W. Bush. By game time he was stretched out on a table in the training room, sick as a dog. No one dared claim that it was food poisoning. The official reason was stomach flu, but Elway is convinced it was the breakfast in the West Wing. Kubiak started the game and engineered a 14–10 Bronco win.

Over the years Kubiak signaled plays to Elway from the sidelines and they developed their own signals. At Gary's retirement roast, Coach Dan Reeves got on Kubiak about the signal for a shovel pass, which was the motion of a man shoveling. Reeves said he couldn't figure out why the play wasn't working, but he understood when he saw the signal.

Not to be outdone, Kubiak told the story of another set of signals. When Reeves put a new play in, Kubiak told Elway when the play was called, he'd grab his balls. The next week, Reeves put in a variation of the play but kept the original in as well. When Kubiak asked Elway how he wanted to distinguish between the two plays, John said, "Grab Dan's balls."

offense, and in 1993 Elway passed for more than 4,000 yards for the first time in his career, had the top quarterback rating in the AFC, was named the AFC's Most Valuable Player, and was the starting quarterback in the Pro Bowl.

While Elway thrived under Phillips, in his two seasons the team struggled. Bowlen fired Phillips and this time when he asked Shanahan, Mike accepted. Discipline and a winning attitude were reestablished.

Denver appeared headed for the Super Bowl after an excellent 1996 season, but it ended when the Broncos were upset by the second-year expansion Jacksonville Jaguars 30–27 at Mile High Stadium. Strangely, Denver had been 13–3 for only the second time in franchise history, only to see the season end in an upset in the first playoff game. This had happened once before, to the Pittsburgh Steelers, 24–17, in 1984.

The Broncos knew they were a good team and the Jacksonville loss gave them incentive for 1997. The defense was among the best in the league, and the offensive was clicking with Elway having a crew of excellent receivers, an all-star running back in Terrell Davis, and the top offensive line in football. The architect of that offensive line was Alex Gibbs. He had been with the Broncos before under Reeves and Shanahan brought him back as assistant head coach and offensive line coach.

After an impressive 11–2 start, Denver lost three of their last four games and went to the playoffs as a wild card team. They got revenge on Jacksonville by beating the Jaguars 42–17.

Getting to the Super Bowl as a wild card team means playing one extra game and playing away from home. They used revenge as motivation against Jacksonville, and their next two games were against teams that had beaten them in the regular season. They beat Kansas City (14–10) and Pittsburgh (24–10) to gain their fifth Super Bowl appearance.

Bronco fans felt no better about Denver's chances against the defending champions, the Green Bay Packers, in the Super Bowl this time than they did earlier in the decade. They

After being on the losing end of three Super Bowls, John Elway finally gets to hoist the Lombardi Trophy after the Broncos beat the Green Bay Packers 31–24 in Super Bowl XXXII. (Courtesy Ryan McKee/Rich Clarkson and Associates)

prepared themselves for another disappointment in San Diego, but the players looked forward to playing the Packers.

Elway finally got his Super Bowl ring, but he didn't have to carry the team. Terrell Davis gained 157 yards, scored three touchdowns, and was the game's MVP. The defense continued its postseason surge and made big plays when needed.

After the Rocky Mountain high of the Super Bowl win waned, reality set in as sure as the winter snow. The major question was Elway. Would he retire? He had his ring; who could blame him? The other question was how many of the Super Bowl champs would be back? Would the free agents cash in on their fame? The answer to the last question first. Eighteen starters said they'd like to try it again in Denver. Two went elsewhere. Gary Zimmerman retired. On June 1 Elway announced he would be back for his sixteenth season.

In 1997 Denver played like the great team it was. The goal was to repeat as NFL champion.

By December the Broncos had the sports world buzzing over the possibility of their becoming only the second undefeated team in NFL history. The Miami Dolphins had accomplished that in 1972, playing a fourteen-game schedule.

The Broncos rolled over their first 13 opponents, with many significant events on the way. Jason Elam tied a twenty-eight-year-old NFL record by kicking a 63-yard field goal. Elway became the second player in NFL history to gain 50,000 yards passing (Dan Marino reached the plateau first) in a win over Oakland, and the Broncos clinched their ninth AFC West title on the final Sunday of November. On December 6 Denver ran its record to 13–0 and tied an NFL record with its eighteenth straight victory, dating back to the previous season. The 13–0 record tied the Chicago Bears feat in 1934 but was second to Miami's 14–0 in 1972.

Alex Gibbs—Master of the Big Men

Alex Gibbs has been a coach for more than forty years and has been on the staff of every team currently in the AFC West.

You might want to duck if you ever call him doctor, but he does have a doctorate in education from Auburn. He studied pre-law at the University of North Carolina and earned a master's degree in European history.

His college coaching career took him to Duke, Kentucky, West Virginia, Ohio State, and back to Auburn before Dan Reeves tapped him to come to Denver in 1984. He played a major role in the Broncos' trips to successive Super Bowls in 1986 and 1987.

In 2001, suffering from burnout, Gibbs asked for relief from full time duties. He stayed with the team during training camp and commuted to Denver from Arizona during the season for the weekend games. As time went on Gibbs found himself with the team more and more. When he was healthy again and wanted to return to full-time, he had been replaced by Rick Dennison, and Mike Shanahan was happy with Dennison's work. Gibbs ended his association with the Broncos when he joined the Atlanta Falcons as offensive line coach in January 2004.

Gibbs is not very big, much shorter and thinner than the group he coaches. He is a tyrant, but his players love him. Veteran guard Mark Schlereth, now retired, said, "He was really hard on us, physically, mentally, and vocally. He was often derogatory. There were times when we hated him, but we always had respect for him, because we knew he respected us and was behind us 100 percent."

Schlereth said, "Alex had no ego problem. He didn't mind changing his philosophy or the techniques if it worked better. If an individual had a better way of getting the job done, he was open to letting him do it. This is unheard of in the coaching profession."

Schlereth continued, "We were a team within the team. We were united. Alex would always take time in meetings to make sure we knew each other well. That built the unity. We were a smaller line, so we didn't overpower people. He taught us better angles and position and teamwork."

In 1995 the linemen started a tradition of not talking to the media

Offensive line coach Alex Gibbs gives directions to his group.
(Courtesy Eric Lars Bakke/Rich Clarkson and Associates)

during the season. Gibbs didn't originate it, but he went along with it, so he wouldn't talk either. Schlereth said, "We really had a ball with that. If a lineman was quoted in the media, there would be a Kangaroo Court, and any fines levied would go into a fund for a postseason party. I paid a lot of fines because I was doing a brief bit during the morning show on KOA. I got away with it for awhile, but they caught me. Tom Nalen did an interview with his hometown newspaper back in Massachusetts, and someone sent it to us. He paid. It was a game for us to see what we could get away with."

The pressure was enormous. Newspaper, radio, and television reporters were dogging the team about the unbeaten season. The last time Denver had lost a football game was on December 15, 1997, in San Francisco. Now it was December 13, 1998, at the Meadowlands in New Jersey. The Broncos scored a season-low sixteen points against the Giants, the only time all year they were held under twenty. New York won 20–16 and the streak was over. The team appeared relieved that the burden of the winning streak had been lifted. They didn't recover the next week and lost at Miami 31–21.

The Broncos had lost three of their last four in 1997 but gained momentum by winning the finale. After going 13–0, then losing two straight, Elway urged his teammates to relax and get the winning feeling again. It worked. Elway tossed 4 touchdown passes and Davis rambled for 178 yards to finish with more than 2,000 yards for the season. The Broncos' 14–2 record was the best in franchise history.

Denver avenged the late season loss to Miami by trouncing the Dolphins in the first round of the playoffs, 38–3. In the AFC Championship Game against the Jets, Denver had problems in the first half. New York took a 10–0 lead when a blocked punt gave them the ball at the Bronco 1, and Curtis Martin took it into the end zone on first down. That was a wake-up call for Denver. Elway made a big play with a 47-yard completion to McCaffrey. It was a play that lent emphasis to Denver's experience. Elway said, "McCaffrey and Rod Smith lined up on the wrong side of the line. I had to yell at them. They simply switched jobs. That play really got us going."

Denver won 23–10.

Elway knew that it was his final game at Mile High. He said, "I'll never forget getting the trophy and carrying it around the stadium, paying tribute to the fans who were so great to me during the sixteen years that I played here. It was kinda my way to say good-bye and look some people in the eye and say, 'Thank you.' "

The Broncos beat the Atlanta Falcons 34–19 in the Super Bowl. Denver had proven it was the best team in football and Elway was named the game's most valuable player.

"If I was to write a book," he told me, "I wouldn't be able to write it with the outcome that I had. I would have thought that would have been too good. It was great to win that game and play as well as we did, get the MVP, and walk off into the sunset."

Success and Conflict: Shanahan, Reeves, and Elway

On January 31, 1995, Mike Shanahan was named the eleventh coach in Broncos history. On January 31, 1999, Shanahan hoisted the Lombardi Trophy above his head as Denver won its second straight Super Bowl. Not bad for four years. Shanahan finally ended the frustration that had plagued Bronco fans for more than 35 years.

When hired, Shanahan was not unknown to Denver, nor was the Bronco organization a mystery to him, having been an assistant in two different stints under Dan Reeves. There ultimately was conflict between Reeves, Shanahan, and quarterback John Elway.

In most disputes of this nature, there are egos involved and unfortunately a lack of communication. No one can question the character of Reeves, Shanahan, and Elway, nor the success each has had in the National Football League.

As one who lived through those years, I will try to tell the story of how it came to a head in the days leading up to Super Bowl XXXIII, when like the perfect storm, the three principals converged on a national stage.

Reeves brought Shanahan to the Broncos from the University of Florida. One of the reasons was to aid Elway's development. After one year he was promoted to offensive coordinator until tapped for his first head coaching job at age thirty-six by none other than Al Davis, managing general partner of the Los Angeles Raiders, Denver's biggest rival. Shanahan was ready to take on a head coaching job, but hardly ready for what he found in Los Angeles.

The veteran Raiders resented the youthful Shanahan, and Davis meddled in the operation of the team. His relationship with Davis deteriorated and after a 7–9 season in 1988 and a 1–3 start the next year, Davis fired Shanahan.

Within days of his firing, Shanahan came back to Denver, only to be fired after the 1991 season by the same guy who brought him back, Dan Reeves. Reeves accused him of collaborating on game plans with Elway and keeping the head coach out of the loop.

Shanahan didn't take on Reeves in the media, but privately said that Dan misinterpreted things and steadfastly maintained that he was not disloyal to his boss. Shanahan went on to success in San Francisco as the offensive coordinator, but Reeves was fired after an 8–8 season in 1992, losing four straight games with Elway on the bench with a shoulder injury.

Reeves's professional background was with the Dallas Cowboys as a player and assistant coach. He became the Broncos head coach in 1981, hired by Edgar Kaiser Jr., who was the new Bronco owner.

John Elway arrived in 1983 in a trade engineered by Kaiser, who then sold the team to Pat Bowlen in 1984, turning a considerable profit. The Reeves–Bowlen team was successful as the Broncos won AFC championships in 1986, 1987, and 1989.

Despite this success the relationship between Elway and Reeves deteriorated. Elway saw wide-open offenses around the NFL and felt he was being held back by an offense that he considered archaic. He witnessed it firsthand in New Orleans at Super Bowl XXIV as Joe Montana, operating the 'Niners "West Coast" offense humiliated the Broncos 55–10. Montana passed for 297 yards and five touchdowns. Elway completed only ten passes for 106 yards and no touchdowns. He was humiliated and embarrassed. To close friends he admitted doubts about his chances of making the Hall of Fame. In a rare selfish moment, he said his numbers would be much better in a different system.

Reeves Missing in Action (but Not for Long)

I n 1990 Denver traveled to Tokyo to play an American Bowl game against Seattle. It was a difficult trip. The heat and humidity in the Japanese capital were stifling. Following the afternoon game in the Tokyo Dome, the team boarded buses for the two-hour trip to the airport, then the fifteen-hour flight to Seattle for refueling, and another three hours plus to Denver. When they dragged themselves off the airplane, it was still Sunday afternoon. It had been a long day.

Everyone in the Bronco organization was exhausted, but Reeves and the coaches went right to work. They had the second preseason game against the Colts in Indianapolis in six days. The Broncos had beaten the Seahawks 10-7, but Reeves saw a lot of things that needed correcting.

A day later, back at camp in Greeley, Reeves went out for his nightly bike ride between dinner and the evening meetings. He felt strange sensations in his shoulder, throat, and chest. His good friend Mike Ditka, the Chicago Bears coach, had suffered a heart attack two years

In 1990 Denver won only five games and Elway's problems with Reeves were mounting. To his credit Elway attempted to keep it private, but he finally did open up to Denver's award-winning columnist, Dick Connor. Connor's column appeared in the *Denver Post* on November 14, 1990. It was entitled, "Friction Not Fiction Between Reeves, Elway."

Elway admitted to Connor that he was unhappy and it was getting worse. Elway told Connor, "We hardly talk to each other unless it's game time." Elway acknowledged that it wasn't all Dan's fault, but he was the only one who could change things. "I'm not easy," Elway told Connor, "but I feel like I've been in the league long enough to know what I feel comfortable with."

earlier, so Reeves knew the symptoms. He went to the hospital. The emergency room doctor administered a stress test and told Reeves that he had not had a heart attack—yet—but that he definitely had a blockage that needed immediate attention. For the first time in his life, the forty-six-year-old Reeves felt vulnerable. Barefoot and with an intravenous solution going into his arm, he was rushed to the Greeley airport where he boarded a private jet for California and immediate surgery.

As reporters huddled at the camp the next day to get the latest information on Reeves' condition, he shocked everyone by walking up to the group outside the Broncos offices. He said he was fine and delighted in relating the procedure. He couldn't remember the name of it (artherectomy), but it was something new. He called it a Roto-Rooter that took plaque out of the arteries. Like a kid showing off his scar, he described the procedure in detail. Everyone cringed when he related how the doctors went in through his groin.

Reeves would not travel to Indianapolis (he named Wade Phillips as the interim coach). He announced that he would change his lifestyle by eating better and dealing with the stress of his job. He was back at practice the next week, but despite his efforts at a lifestyle change, those health problems continue to plague him today.

In 1991 Reeves gave Elway more input into the game plans and included him in the planning meetings. As a successful season wore on, Elway was having less input, and after losing the AFC Championship Game to Buffalo, the rift intensified when Reeves fired Shanahan.

There were rumors of an Elway trade to the Washington Redskins. Elway was convinced they were true. Bowlen quickly put a damper on the speculation, saying that he would not allow that to happen.

If the trade talks were a blow to Elway, the 1992 draft hit him like a sledgehammer. Elway asked Reeves for help in the offensive line and for a big-play receiver. Such a receiver, Carl Pickens of Tennessee, was on the board when Denver came up with the twenty-fifth pick of the draft. Reeves selected quarterback Tommy Maddox, who had just completed his sophomore season at UCLA. Maddox had excellent credentials—first team All-American and the only Pac-10 player to have gone past 5,000 yards passing in his first two years. But why did the Broncos draft a quarterback? Not only had Reeves not heeded Elway's request, but talked about the post-Elway era. Elway, who correctly believed he had good years left, began to question his future in Denver.

Denver's record was 7–3 in 1992, when Elway suffered a shoulder injury that would sideline him for four games. Reeves now faced a situation of his own making without an experienced backup at quarterback. There was the raw rookie, Maddox, and a second-year quarterback from Virginia with no experience in the NFL, Shawn Moore. The Broncos lost all four games and one thing was evident—the team was not the same without Elway.

Elway returned and got a win, making the playoffs a possibility with a win in the finale at Kansas City. The mistake-

Did Reeves Realize That He Was Going to Be Fired?

I'm not sure Dan really believed this would happen. I spent some time with Dan and his wife, Pam, in their hotel suite in Kansas City the day before that final game. They were concerned, but deep down I think Dan felt that he was going to weather the storm. I was not as optimistic. On more than one occasion during that season, a high-ranking Broncos executive had hinted that a change had to be made. I was even asked which of the two, Elway or Reeves, could the Broncos least afford to lose. Others in the team offices were hostile toward Reeves behind the scenes. There was a morale problem in the organization. Bowlen realized he had to do something.

Some say Elway pressured Bowlen to make the change. Elway insisted he had no input. Bowlen confirmed it. He said, "John's a player, and players don't make those decisions."

In the end I think Bowlen felt that the Broncos simply needed a new direction. Yet, when asked what would he have done with Reeves if Elway had not been injured, and the Broncos had gone on to another outstanding season, he answered, "Extend his contract."

prone Broncos lost to the Chiefs 42–20 and the next day Bowlen fired Reeves. Dan's Denver career was over with a record of 116–78–1.

Bowlen wanted Shanahan, but Mike declined. Bowlen hired defensive coordinator Wade Phillips. His two years at the helm were not successful. Again, Bowlen asked Shanahan and this time Mike accepted.

After the "relaxed" style of Coach Phillips, the Broncos were back to discipline. Meetings and practices were meticulously planned, executed, and on time. Shanahan expanded his coaching staff and demanded dedication from his assistants. Media access to practice and the players was controlled. No stone was left unturned.

Shanahan expects his organization and his players to live up to his standards of mental toughness, focus, and effort. He has an excellent relationship with his boss and has complete control over the football operation including salaries, personnel, management of the salary cap, and so on. Shanahan is known for his offensive genius, but he's equally astute on the defensive side. He monitors every aspect of the game plan throughout the week.

Shanahan retooled the Broncos and led them to their first world championship in 1997, advancing through the playoffs as a wild card team.

The team was exceptional in 1998, rolling to a 13–0 record. There was talk of an undefeated season, but losses in New York and Miami ended those dreams. However, Denver was not to be denied its second straight Super Bowl, beating the Dolphins 38–3 and the Jets 23–10 to win the AFC championship again.

Shanahan coached the Broncos to successive seasons of 13–3, 12–4, and 14–2, with the last two ending in Super Bowl championships, but things have not gone as well since. Elway retired and Shanahan placed the offense in the hands of Brian Griese, who quarterbacked Michigan to the national collegiate championship. Griese had a Pro Bowl year in 2000, but Denver lost 21–3 to Baltimore in the playoffs. Shanahan flirted with returning to Florida as head coach after the 2001 season but stayed in Denver.

Just prior to the 2003 campaign, Shanahan was rewarded with a contract extension that will take him through the 2008 season. It made him the highest-paid coach in the NFL. But some of the glow is wearing off; Shanahan gave up on Griese and signed former Arizona Cardinal quarterback Jake Plummer. Plummer suffered through a so-so season, punctuated by injuries as second-year running back Clinton Portis emerged as the key man on offense. Denver finished with a 10–6 record and played in the 2003–2004 season Wild Card game at Indianapolis. It was only the second playoff appearance since Elway's retirement, and Peyton Manning and the Colts took the Broncos apart in a 41–10 victory. After the season Shanahan shocked fans by trading Portis, who was the NFL's Offensive Rookie of the Year.

Reeves was making some history of his own. After being fired in Denver, he was named head coach of the New York Giants in 1993 and had instant success with an 11–5 record, but the next three years were not as productive and he was fired after the 1996 season. He returned home to Georgia as coach of the Falcons. His 1998 Falcons finished 14–2. He missed part of the December schedule because of open-heart surgery. He was back on the bench for the playoffs as the Falcons beat San Francisco 20–18 in an NFC divisional playoff game and upset the Minnesota Vikings 30–27 in overtime to win the NFC Championship Game.

The circle was complete. Three paths arrived at the same point at the same time. Reeves, Shanahan, and Elway would meet in Miami in the Super Bowl. The football world waited to see what would happen and it didn't have to wait long.

Reeves and Elway had exchanged barbs the season after he was fired. Elway said he wasn't enjoying football under Reeves. Elway said, "The first six or seven years were okay, but the last three years have been hell. I felt like [the Reeves staff] never did anything offensively to make us better."

Dan Reeves coaching the Atlanta Falcons against Mike Shanahan and John Elway in Super Bowl XXXIII. Atlanta took a 3–0 lead but lost the game to Denver 34–19. (Courtesy David Gonzales/Rich Clarkson and Associates)

Reeves, then the Giants coach, shot back, "Let's just say it wasn't heaven for me either. I hope maybe one of these days he'll grow up and mature a little."

There seemed to be some efforts at reconciliation. Reeves had made a point of congratulating Shanahan on Denver's first Super Bowl win at the scouting combine and had played golf with Mike at the owner's meeting. Later, all three played golf at Augusta National in the week prior to the Masters. Were things patched up?

Following the championship games, the teams spent the first week working at their own headquarters, but media from both cities were present in Atlanta and Denver. The questions started and Reeves slipped first (or maybe not as we'll learn later). He said the wounds of his firing in Denver still hadn't healed and one of the protagonists was Shanahan. Reeves said, "The biggest problem I had was that if John Elway had a problem with me and you're coaching the position, why did I not know prior to reading about it in the paper?"

From Denver, Shanahan countered, "I thought we were both going to take the high road on this. Dan Reeves knew his relationship with John. There's no ifs, ands, or buts about it. It was a tough relationship from the second year, from the first year. Everybody in this town knows that."

The war of words had started. Reeves said he felt his authority as head coach was being challenged, and added, "When I fired Mike, I knew it wasn't going to help the relationship with John. I knew they were really good friends and still are, but if I was going to do what I thought was best, I had to go ahead and make that decision."

Back in Denver, Shanahan said, "Dan wanted to run the offense and he wanted complete control. He didn't want somebody with my type of personality around. Dan was probably one of my closest friends at the time. Any time you end the way we did, there's a little on the inside of you that rubs each of us the wrong way. But we're both mature enough to handle it."

The rhetoric continued through the week, but softened. Elway said, "It was a tough time for everybody. It's one of those things you wish didn't have to happen, but it did, and nobody can change what happened there. Bygones are bygones and that was six years ago. I've moved on and I concentrate on the good times. The focus has been on the bad times, but we had a hell of a lot more good times than bad times. Time cures a lot of problems. Some things don't seem so important or as big a deal as they did at the time. Time moves on."

Reeves began to say kind things about Elway. "He was great to coach," Dan said, "I thought he was a great quarterback. When you coach somebody as long as I coached John, you realize what a great quarterback he is and was."

And as for Shanahan, Reeves said, "Mike knew how to get the best out of him. There was just a respect there and it's obviously still there."

The worst was over. Shanahan seemed to put an end to it when he said, "This game, as I've said before, is much bigger than Mike Shanahan or Dan Reeves. It's everything we've been working for from a team standpoint."

The issue indeed died when the teams moved to Miami. There were new media members asking the same questions, but the principals refused to answer, referring reporters to their statements of the previous week.

Some believe Reeves intentionally fired the first volley to get it out in the open and out of the way. Falcons wide receiver James Lofton said, "If you're waging a war, this is a great preemptive first strike . . . that's old news now. If he planned this, I think it was a good move."

Broncos tight end Shannon Sharpe agreed, "Obviously, this has been eating at Dan for a long time, and this is something he felt he had to get off his chest. Maybe now, we can move past that."

Super Bowl XXXIII belonged to the Broncos, who won handily, 34–19. Elway was spectacular, passing for 336 yards and a touchdown and scoring another himself. He was voted the game's most valuable player. In postgame comments, there was no gloating, but make no mistake about it. It was a satisfying win for Shanahan and Elway.

An intense Mike Shanahan on the sidelines at Super Bowl XXXIII. It was a satisfying win for Mike over his old boss, Dan Reeves. (Courtesy Ryan McKee/Rich Clarkson and Associates)

Elway retired and was inducted into the Colorado Sports Hall of Fame. Reeves followed him a couple of years later. Shanahan's turn will come.

On December 10, 2003, with three games remaining in the season, Dan Reeves was fired for the third time in his career. Reeves asked to be released immediately when informed by Atlanta owner Arthur Blank that he would be dismissed following the season.

The circumstances that led to his firing were hauntingly familiar. In 1992 the Broncos were 7–3, when John Elway was injured and missed four games, all of which Denver lost. The team ultimately finished 8–8 and Reeves was fired.

At Atlanta, Reeves had another "franchise" quarterback in Michael Vick, but the optimism going into the 2003 season was dashed when Vick was injured at the start of the season and the Falcons fell to 3–10 before he returned. So both times an injured star quarterback led to Dan's demise.

In another touch of irony, Wade Phillips replaced Reeves as interim coach with the Falcons. Reeves had hired Phillips as defensive coordinator after Phillips lost his head coaching job at Buffalo. He was hired by Reeves as defensive coordinator of the Broncos in 1990 and replaced Reeves as head coach at Denver after Dan lost his job there.

It's probable that Shanahan and Reeves will never return to their former relationship, but as for Elway, in a recent conversation, he said that now that he no longer plays and has had an opportunity to reflect, that the relationship he had with Reeves wasn't as strained as some people made it out to be. He said, "Sure we didn't agree on everything, but we were pretty good for each other. We won a lot of football games."

John Elway of Denver—A Football Legend

J
ohn Elway had just done it again. It was another legendary comeback and my broadcast partner, Dave Logan, exclaimed, "I tell you, they ought to knight this guy." If Colorado were a kingdom, John wouldn't be a knight, he'd be the king.

The State of Colorado has a team in all of the major professional sports, with hockey heroes such as Patrick Roy, Joe Sakic, and Peter Forsburg. They led the way to the Stanley Cup in 1996 and 2002. In baseball the Rockies had the Blake Street Bombers: Larry Walker, Dante Bichette, Andres Galarraga, and Vinny Castilla. The Nuggets had David Thompson and Dan Issel. Elway stands above them all. Sportswriter Dave Socier wrote in the *Pueblo Chieftain*, "Elway became more famous than Colorado's superb ski slopes."

Elway is the first Denver Bronco to be inducted into the Pro Football Hall of Fame, in 2004, his first year of eligibility. It took Denver forty-four years to get a bust in Canton. Other Broncos certainly deserve it, but because it worked out that way, it is fitting that Elway be the first.

When his election was announced at the Super Bowl in February 2004, Elway remembered his first start against the

Steelers, where he completed only one pass and was running for his life before being replaced in the second half. Elway remembers, "I thought, 'What in the hell have I gotten myself into?' I didn't want to look across the line at Jack Lambert drooling and wild-eyed. I wanted to click my heels and say, 'Auntie Em take me home' "

This is the story of the man in that football uniform. John has never been caught up in his own importance. He has always had time for people. He graciously honors autograph requests. Through his Elway Foundation he returns millions of dollars to the community in charitable projects. I have been privileged to describe most of John's feats on the football field, but I consider it a bigger privilege to call him a friend.

As John settles into midlife, things have not been easy. In a span of two years, 2001 and 2002, his father and best friend, Jack, died; his twin sister, Jana, lost her battle with cancer; and he was divorced from his wife, Janet.

John and Janet met at Stanford, where she was a world-class swimmer and led the Cardinal to the NCAA championship in 1980. Her athletic background helped her understand what John had to adjust to as Colorado's most recognized citizen. John and Janet were blessed with four great kids: daughters, Jessica, Jordan, and Juliana and a son, Jack.

John's most cherished moments were and still are the time he spends with his children. John was still playing when Jack started playing Little League football. John's instructions were that his son play in the offensive line so he could learn what football was really about. Not surprisingly, Jack ended up at quarterback. When John retired, he coached the team.

John's love of kids extends to others. The Broncos were playing the Colts in a preseason game in Indianapolis. Because the Hoosier Dome was only 2 blocks from the hotel, the players

John's Best Friend

Jack and John Elway, father and son, were truly best friends. Jack had a long coaching career in high school, college, and professional ranks. He was coaching in Port Angeles, Washington, when the twins, John and Jana, were born in 1960.

John learned offensive football at an early age from the master. Most acknowledge that the origins and principles of the "West Coach Offense" started with Jack Elway.

Jack was the head coach at San Jose State and found himself on the opposite sideline from his son, when the Spartans played Stanford. I once asked John why he didn't go to San Jose to play for his dad. John said he wasn't asked. Jack agrees. "I had to be the dumbest coach in America," Jack told me. "There I have the best quarterback in America sitting at my dinner table every night, and I let him go to a school right up the street in Palo Alto."

One of Jack's biggest victories was bittersweet. San Jose beat the Cardinal 28–6 in 1981, John's junior year. But Jack did get to coach John on the college level—in the East–West Shrine Game, and John ended up being the game's offensive MVP.

After John's rookie year in Denver, Jack became Stanford's coach through the 1988 season. After that, he did some pro scouting and coached the Frankfurt Galaxy in the World League of American Football. John spent time with his dad during the spring and summer seasons in Germany and was elated to find that he could walk the streets and go to the beer halls with no one recognizing him. It was a special time for the Elways.

The two were together again when Jack joined the Broncos in 1993 as a scout; he later headed up the scouting operation before retiring.

I loved talking to Jack—about football, about John, about life. It's not hard to understand the love that John had for his dad.

One of Jack's best friends was Jerry Frei, who had been a head coach at Oregon, an assistant in the NFL, and a scout for the Broncos. Jack liked his vodka martinis and he and Jerry were known to relax by tipping a few together. Jerry died just weeks before Jack. John quipped at his father's memorial service, that he imagined the two of them in heaven having that nightly martini.

walked there for a warm-up on the morning of the game. Elway stayed with me to tape the pregame show after his teammates departed. When we left the Dome for the walk back to the hotel, a young boy was waiting. John not only signed his card, but also struck up a conversation that continued for the duration of the walk back to the hotel. I suspect this young man will never forget his stroll with a legend.

When the Broncos played the Seattle Seahawks in Tokyo in 1990, I was on the same bus as Elway going to the first practice session on the grounds near the Olympic Stadium. When we arrived, hundreds of Japanese children greeted us, chanting, "Eh-way, Eh-way." John was mobbed as he left the bus. He had tears in his eyes as he waded through the kids, touching as many hands as he could. It's one of the treasured images that I have of Elway.

There are many stories illustrating Elway's human side. One of my favorites is the one told by Broncos Vice President of Public Relations Jim Saccamano. The Broncos were in Wisconsin to play the Green Bay Packers and were quartered in a hotel in Appleton. Meetings were scheduled shortly after check-in. Elway was making his way through the group of autograph seekers, signing as many notebooks, papers, and napkins as he could. When he finally made it to the elevator, he shared it with a young lady who instantly recognized him. She excitedly explained that she was a bridesmaid and that the reception was underway at the hotel. She pleaded with him to come to the reception and say hello to the bride and groom. Elway declined and explained that he had to go to a meeting.

As it turned out the meeting waited. John went back downstairs and to the wedding reception and posed for pictures with the bride and groom. Why? John explained that he felt guilty for declining the invitation.

I was honored to make the induction speech when John joined the Colorado Sports Hall of Fame. It was one of the most emotional moments of my life. I spoke from my heart. The Elway table was in front of the podium, and there were many hankies going to the eyes. John struggled through his acceptance speech. People at that banquet saw that human, emotional side of John, which was rarely revealed in public.

John had many tearful moments as he approached his retirement announcement. On Sunday, May 2, 1999, with the nation watching, John bid a tearful farewell to football. His retirement announcement was scheduled two weeks earlier, but when the worst school shooting in U.S. history occurred at Columbine High School in Littleton, Elway postponed the announcement and mourned with the rest of Denver.

I retain many images of John Elway. The low point was the morning after the Super Bowl in New Orleans, where in a head to head battle with Joe Montana and the 49ers, the Broncos were humiliated 55–10. I was seated next to John and Janet on the charter returning to Denver. There was nothing that could be said or done that would console him. He was unhappy with his coach, he was a three-time Super Bowl loser, and he feared his place in football history would not be realized.

Elway came to the NFL after three All-American seasons at Stanford. He was the number one player taken in the draft, which included other outstanding quarterbacks (Dan Marino, Jim Kelly, Tony Eason, Ken O'Brien, and Todd Blackledge), all taken in the first round.

The Baltimore Colts had the top pick, but Elway made it clear that he wanted to play on the West Coast, and if that didn't happen, he would give up football and play baseball. He had played one season in the New York Yankees organization

In his rookie season John Elway had a lot to learn. Here (seated) he studies a play chart with veteran quarterback Steve DeBerg. (Courtesy Rich Clarkson/Rich Clarkson and Associates)

at Class A Oneonta, New York. Even though Yankees owner George Steinbrenner compared him with a young Mickey Mantle, John enjoyed only moderate success. But Colts coach Frank Kush couldn't make a blockbuster deal for the draft rights to Elway, so he drafted him.

Kush was convinced that Elway really wanted to play football and was willing to wait him out. Owner, Robert Irsay Jr., was not and made a deal with Denver. Baltimore got an outstanding offensive tackle, Chris Hinton, who was Denver's top pick (Hinton had many All-Pro years in the NFL), backup quarterback Mark Hermann, Denver's top 1984 draft pick, and a million dollars. The Broncos not only robbed the bank, but took the Brinks truck as well.

The youthful Elway came to Denver and quickly learned that his life wasn't his own. At his first training camp in Greeley, he was greeted by a horde of local and national newspaper and radio/television reporters. The "Elway Watch" was on: What Elway wore, what Elway ate, what he said to a coach, what he said to a teammate, when he got a haircut, and on and on, were endlessly reported. One sports cartoonist drew a classic of Elway going into a stall in the men's room only to find a camera sticking out of the toilet.

Elway survived and played sixteen years for Denver, leading the Broncos to 7 AFC West championships, 22 postseason games (14 wins, 8 losses), 6 AFC Championship Games (5 wins, 1 loss), and 5 Super Bowls (2 wins, 3 losses). When he retired, he had put together a string of seven straight postseason wins, including the two Super Bowl victories.

I remember Elway, airborne and spinning his way to a critical first down inside the Packer 10 yard line. The play has become known as "The Helicopter." Shannon Sharpe was quoted in *Sports Illustrated* as saying, "When I saw him do that

"He's Not the Kind of Guy You Win Championships With"

The trade that brought Elway to the Broncos was cause to celebrate in the Mile High City. Not so around the rest of football. Sportswriters and fans around the country were calling him names—"spoiled brat," "juvenile," "overrated." Perhaps the most scathing comments came from the Hall of Fame quarterback of the Pittsburgh Steelers, Terry Bradshaw.

Bradshaw said, "So he didn't want to go to a team that needed his services. The thing about the National Football League is that the team with the worst record gets an opportunity to improve by picking the best player and Elway going to Baltimore would have helped them a lot. By him saying, 'I don't want to do that,' is a slap in the face for the draft and the National Football League. I could have come out of Louisiana when I was the first player picked saying, 'I don't want to go up to Pittsburgh, it's ugly, it's cold, the people don't understand a southern boy, and I want to be close to my momma.' I could have done the same thing, but I didn't, I went, and why I went was because they were 1–13 and I said I'm going to go up there and make them a winner, and we did. . . . For a guy like Elway to say, 'I want to be on the West Coast. I want to be on the beach. I'm a California boy.' Well, who cares what you are? Then he says, 'I'll play baseball.' Play baseball. He should play baseball, because in my opinion he's not the kind of guy you win championships with. He never did it when he was at Stanford and I don't think he will do it in Denver. Personally, I don't care if he never does it."

In a touch of irony, Bradshaw was anchoring coverage from the field stage in San Diego and Miami after the Broncos had won back-to-back Super Bowls and did the postgame interviews with Elway. By then, John and Terry had buried the hatchet, but when Bradshaw originally spoke out, Elway was stung by those words when he was doing what he thought was best for himself.

John Elway with Terry Bradshaw (right) holds the Lombardi Trophy after the Broncos beat Atlanta in Super Bowl XXXIII.
(Courtesy Ryan McKee/Rich Clarkson and Associates)

John Elway goes airborne to pick up extra yards inside the Green Bay 10 yard line in Super Bowl XXXII. The play, nick-named "The Helicopter," was an inspiration for his teammates. (Courtesy Ryan McKee/Rich Clarkson and Associates)

and then get up pumping his fist, I was sure we were going to win." It was the third quarter. The score was 17–17. Third and 6 at the Green Bay 12. As Elway had done so many times, when receivers were covered, he ran for it. He was close to a first down and could have run out of bounds, but he wanted more and headed up the sidelines. He took one shot that knocked him into the air and another while he was in the air. When he landed at the 4, he had the first down. Denver scored two plays later. After the game, grasping the Lombardi Trophy, team owner Bowlen exclaimed, "This one is for John."

I remember after what John knew was his final game at Mile High Stadium, a 23–10 win over the New York Jets, he walked around the stadium waving at the fans and screaming over the public address system, "I love you."

I remember Elway scoring the final touchdown against Atlanta in the Super Bowl in Miami. When the camera zoomed in, there was Elway lying on the goal line with the ball in the end zone and guard Mark Schlereth on top of him. John's grin was as wide as the Grand Canyon.

I remember Elway on the podium hoisting the Lombardi Trophy and the MVP Award. The Broncos had beaten the Atlanta Falcons, coached by Dan Reeves. John had purged his last demon. It was his happiest moment in football.

John Elway, Where You Get an Honest Deal

It's difficult, even today, to not be aware of John Elway. He is on television many times a day selling cars for one of the many dealerships that bear his name.

John graduated from Stanford with a degree in economics and is successful in the automobile business. He first became a partner in a dealership with Bronco owner Pat Bowlen.

Elway later partnered with veteran dealer Rod Buscher and built an empire. The partnership was a good one. Buscher knew the business and Elway had a name, money, and a good business head on his shoulders. John followed through on his commitment to take care of the customer.

Elway didn't let his business interests slide during the season. He established his office at one of the dealerships close to the Bronco Complex. He would stop there on his way to practice or on his way home. He became a fixture on the television screens by pushing his own product, mostly in a light-hearted way.

Elway and Buscher sold the business to a national chain, but the seventeen Colorado dealerships retain Elway's name. John is still active in management and remains the commercial spokesman.

Elway yearned to get back into football as an executive, but he wanted a decision-making position. That wasn't possible with the Broncos. Mike Shanahan controlled the football operation. Elway joined a group that made an unsuccessful attempt to establish an NFL franchise in Los Angeles.

Elway is now a partner in the ownership of the Colorado Crush in the Arena Football League. He is the chairman and CEO and manages the everyday operation of the team.

The Game of Football Is Not Always Fair

A Hall of Fame career is not recognized. An injury cuts short a career. Professional football can be unfair.

It took forty-four years for Denver to get its first player into the Pro Football Hall of Fame. There wasn't much doubt about John Elway. What about Floyd Little? As is practice in baseball, a player who has not been elected to the Hall during his period of eligibility goes into the list considered by the Veteran's Committee. Floyd's only hope now is as an old-timer.

As for the others. . .

Randy Gradishar

What about Randy Gradishar? Look at the statistics and you'll see that Gradishar ranks with the best linebackers to play in the National Football League. In the 2003 Hall of Fame voting, Gradishar made the final ten for the first time. So, there is still hope.

The Champion, Ohio, native was an All-American at Ohio State. His coach, the late, legendary Woody Hayes, called him "the best defensive player I every coached."

Randy did it all. He was the anchor of the Orange Crush defense and the prototype inside middle linebacker in the 3–4. He is still Denver's all-time leading tackler (2,049). He never missed a game, playing in 145 consecutive contests. He is credited with thirty-three career turnovers (twenty interceptions and thirteen fumble recoveries). One of Gradishar's greatest moments was in his home state against the Cleveland Browns, when he scooped up a low pass and returned the interception 93 yards for a Denver touchdown, the winning points in the game. He was chosen the 1978 NFL Defensive Player of the Year and seven times was elected to the Pro Bowl.

Gradishar was a leader of the 1977 Broncos team that went to the Super Bowl.

His former teammate, Tom Jackson, never one to mince words, said the fact that Randy is not in the Hall of Fame is "stupid." Jackson said, "He's as good a player as this league has ever had."

Gradishar defensive coordinator, Joe Collier, agrees. Collier points out that Gradishar was an every-down man. He didn't come out on passing downs. He was just as effective in dropping back in pass coverage as he was against the run.

Buffalo Bills offensive guard Joe DeLamilleure was elected to the Hall in the 2003 vote. He couldn't believe Gradishar didn't make it. He said, "Without a doubt Randy Gradishar should be in the Hall of Fame. I played against Randy in college and pro ball. Being an offensive guard, I went head to head with Randy. He was, along with Jack Lambert, the best linebacker that I ever played against."

Linebacker Randy Gradishar was the heart and soul of the Orange Crush defense. (Courtesy Rich Clarkson and Associates)

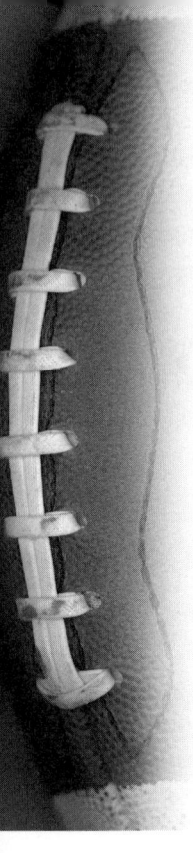

A Leader and a Prankster

Randy Gradishar might be the only person who can say he dumped cold water on John Elway.

When you covered the Broncos at training camp in Greeley, you always wanted to find out where Gradishar's room was in the dorm. You didn't want to walk under it. Randy was an instigator of practical jokes and was deadly in dropping water balloons from his window. The celebrated rookie, John Elway, learned that when he was a target and Gradishar scored a direct hit.

His teammates love to tell another story about Randy. He had the reputation of being frugal. His teammates simply said he "was tight." In one game, as the opponent came to the line of scrimmage, his teammates noticed him leave his position, walk a few steps, pick something out of the grass and slip it into his sock. When asked about it after the game, he said, "I saw a quarter and I wasn't going to let it lay there."

Coach John Ralston said, "I've never seen a more gifted and talented athlete." Coach Red Miller said he was "the most dependable player the Broncos had." From Coach Dan Reeves: "He was as good a linebacker as I have ever been around and I have been around some great ones."

Gradishar surprised everyone when he announced his retirement while still at the top of the game after the 1983 season. But that was Randy. He told me that he had been fortunate to stay healthy and that he wanted to quit before he had to worry about his knees and shoulders for the rest of his life.

He has been inducted into the Colorado Sports Hall of Fame and the Broncos Ring of Fame. He has also been elected to the National Football Foundation Hall of Fame and is a member of College Football's All-Century Team but the Pro Football of Fame continues to elude him. Gradishar made the final group in 2003 but was not elected. He failed to reach the finals in 2004.

Gary Zimmerman

Another former Bronco who should make the Hall of Fame is offensive tackle Gary Zimmerman. Zim spent five productive years with the Broncos after a stellar seven-year career with the Minnesota Vikings. He anchored an offensive line that finally was able to give John Elway protection and open holes to produce a powerful running game. It was this balance that led Denver to two world championships. He was named to the All-NFL team four times, was the NFL Lineman of the Year in 1987, and was selected to the All-Decade teams of the 1980s and the 1990s.

Like Gradishar, Zimmerman was an iron man. After spending time in the USFL, he came to the NFL, where he missed only two games in twelve years, played in 184 games, and started 169 straight. He modestly describes himself as a durable guy who could play hurt. One of the best-kept secrets of the 1997 Super Bowl season was the pain with which Zimmerman played. Zimmerman couldn't lift his arms above shoulder level because of the injuries to his shoulders. Nevertheless, he opened the holes for Terrell Davis who was the game's MVP. Zim stayed out of the weight room because he couldn't lift weights due to his injury. He admits he got a lot done in games on his reputation alone. He is permanently scarred with shoulders that will never be normal.

He didn't stick around for Denver's second Super Bowl win because he couldn't, although Elway tried to talk him into it. Zimmerman attends the huge Harley-Davidson Rally in Sturgis, South Dakota, each summer, and Elway traveled to Sturgis to try to make him reconsider. Zimmerman said that John got him fired-up, but he just knew he couldn't play another year.

He retired to his secluded acreage near Bend, Oregon, where he spends his time cutting trees, fishing, and enjoying his family, happy to be far from the spotlight.

Zimmerman was inducted into the Broncos Ring of Fame in 2003. In an induction speech Elway called him the best left tackle to ever play the game, a sentiment echoed by many others around the NFL. Elway had hoped Zim would join him in the Hall of Fame's 2004 class but although he made the finals, Zimmerman was not one of the four elected. His time will come.

Terrell Davis

In the early days of training camp in 2003, Mike Shanahan had to make the difficult decision to waive running back Terrell Davis. The MVP of Super Bowl XXXII battled injuries to both legs for the last four years of his career, playing in only seventeen games. His first four years were just the opposite. They were spectacular.

Davis was a sixth-round draft choice from Georgia, who quickly caught the eye of all at the Broncos training camp in

Offensive tackle Gary Zimmerman is called by many "the best left tackle to play the game." (Courtesy Eric Lars Bakke/Rich Clarkson and Associates)

1995. He won the starting job and gained 1,117 yards in his rookie season. His yardage increased in each of the next three seasons, climaxed by a sensational 2,008 yards in 1998 when he was voted the NFL's Most Valuable Player, making him only one of nine players to win the league and Super Bowl MVP honors.

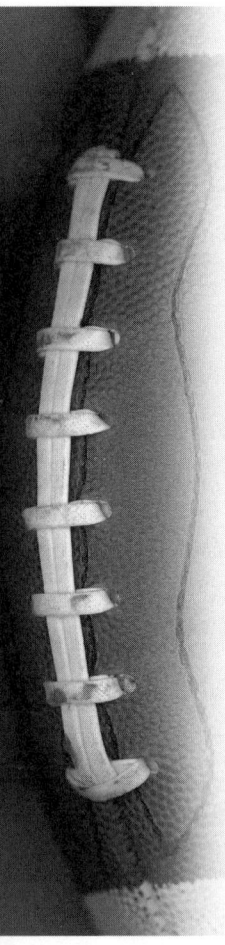

A Real Headache

By midseason in his rookie year, it was obvious that Terrell Davis was something special. Denver finally had a running back to complement John Elway's passing.

He was off to a great start in a game at Mile High Stadium but was on the bench in the heat of the game. Our sideline reporter checked and learned that he had a headache and couldn't continue.

Examinations after the game revealed that Davis had a chronic migraine condition, not life threatening, but certainly severe enough to limit his playing when the headaches developed during a game.

Denver's media produced more information about migraine headaches than you needed or wanted to know. Meanwhile, Terrell's mailbox overflowed with remedies. Everyone had the right solution. The medical staff came up with medication that helped, but never totally prevented, the headaches.

In Super Bowl XXXII, playing in his hometown of San Diego, Davis was named the MVP, and his numbers are even more amazing when you consider he sat out most of the second quarter with a migraine. He gained 157 yards and had a Super Bowl record 3 rushing touchdowns, including the winning points with 1:45 remaining.

Most impressive is the fact that in the seventy-eight games in his short career, he is the Broncos all-time leading rusher, the leader in rushing attempts, rushing touchdowns, and total touchdowns.

Davis started the "salute" after touchdowns that became famous during the Broncos 1997 run to the Super Bowl title, and off the field he created the Terrell Davis Salute the Kids Foundation in Denver and San Diego. It provided financial support to the YMCA, the Boys and Girls Clubs, and Outreach Programs for the Homeless.

Imagine the career numbers Davis could have had if the knee and ankle injuries hadn't limited his career to four productive seasons.

Richard "Tombstone" Jackson

Richard "Tombstone" Jackson is another who had a severe knee injury force him out of football after only six years with the Broncos. Many considered him the best defensive end in professional football during his prime. He was the first Bronco to be named to the All-NFL first team in 1970.

Jackson was nicknamed "Tombstone" because when he slammed into a quarterback or running back, it was the end of the line. Richard was a mountain of a man with the quickness of a cat. He looked mean. He had fierce eyes and a Fu Manchu mustache. Richard exploited this image on the field. His teammate Lyle Alzado said, "I'd be on the other side of the line and I'd hear him talking. He'd say to the lineman across from him, 'I'm gonna knock your head off. I'm comin' boy . . . here I come . . . hear my footsteps?' That offensive lineman's eyes would get real big and Rich would knock him to the ground. Nobody could handle him. He was that powerful. I

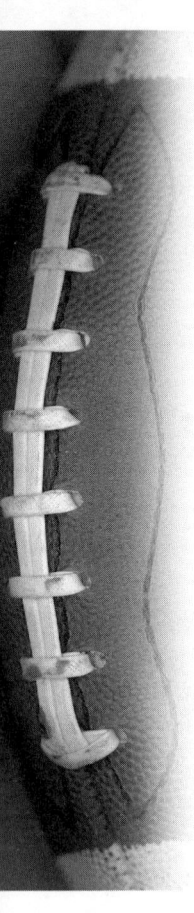

Tombstone's Head Slap Leads to a Rule Change

Rich Jackson invented the head slap. It was no simple maneuver. He explained the variations. "I had the halo spinner," he said, "It came off the head slap. I would go inside the lineman and up the pipe. I also had the bulldog move. I would make a motion with my left hand, slam him with my right, and there's the quarterback sitting there like a duck in the pond. I also used the double head slap. That would give them a headache."

All-Pro offensive tackle of the Oakland Raiders and later the head coach, Art Shell, said of the head slap, "He could split a helmet. He could turn a game by himself. He hit me the hardest that anybody hit me aside the head. It was like a mule kicking me. You never let an opponent know he hurt you, but when he hit me, all I could see was stars. I could barely make it back to the huddle."

Near the end of Jackson's career, the NFL Rules Committee outlawed the maneuver.

saw him pick up tackles and throw them out of the way. Once he had his hands on you, it was over."

Perhaps, the best tribute to Jackson's football career came from Raiders owner Al Davis, who said, "He's one of those players who come to professional football, who is truly great, but will only get the recognition from his peers and only in memory. Richard Jackson was one of the great players in the National Football League."

Tom Jackson

Another Jackson who won't get to the Hall of Fame is Tom, but he was consistently voted the most inspirational player by his teammates. TJ was the soul of the Orange Crush. When the team needed a lift, Jackson was there to provide it. He played with spirit and enthusiasm and it was infectious. He was a cheerleader on the sidelines, not only with his teammates, but with the fans.

He had a long career and played in 191 games, second only to John Elway. TJ was a big play guy and had some of his best games in Denver's 1977 run to the Super Bowl.

Coach Red Miller always said, "Tom is the only player I know who likes to practice."

Charley Johnson

Then there's Charley Johnson, who was in the twilight of his career when he came to Denver, having won fame with the Cardinals and Oilers. Charley led Denver to its first winning season and brought a winning attitude to the Broncos. He once passed for 445 yards in a game and threw a touchdown pass in ten consecutive contests.

Karl Mecklenburg

Karl Mecklenburg will have a shot at the Hall of Fame. He was one of the second-generation linebackers in the Crush. He had a twelve-year career after being drafted in the twelfth round in 1983 from Minnesota. He became a starter in his third season and went on to start 141 of his 180 games. He played in six Pro Bowls and was the AFC Player of the Year, picked by *Football News*, in 1986.

Linebacker Karl Mecklenburg, a twelfth-round draft choice, played in six Pro Bowls. (Courtesy Rich Clarkson and Associates)

His defensive coach Joe Collier said of Mecklenburg, "He was a versatile player. You could move him around all over the place. He was smart. He could play the defensive line position. He could play inside or outside linebacker and we did move him around a lot. Not many guys could do what he did."

Shannon Sharpe and Rod Smith are still playing. Both have a great chance of following Elway into the Hall of Fame.

Shannon Sharpe

Shannon Sharpe is another example of a late-round draft pick (seventh round) from a small school (Savannah State) who made it big with the Broncos. He came to Denver in 1990 and helped them to their two Super Bowl wins. He signed with Baltimore as an unrestricted free agent in 2000 and helped the Ravens win a Super Bowl. After one more season with the Ravens, he returned to Denver in 2002.

Sharpe is the NFL's all-time leader in receptions and receiving yards by a tight end, and going into 2003, he ranked number one in Bronco history in receptions and second in receiving yards and receiving touchdowns. He has played in 157 games as a Bronco.

Shannon played the early part of his career in the shadow of his brother Sterling, who starred at Green Bay, but now he is recognized as one of the top tight ends to have played in the NFL.

Sharpe is a favorite of the fans and the media. He has a great sense of humor, has a way with words, and is very quotable. New England fans are still infuriated over his sideline antics when Denver was trouncing the Patriots in 1996. Playing to the crowd and taking a cue from history, he grabbed a sideline phone and yelled, "Send in the militia, send in the National Guard, the Broncos are coming, it's a massacre."

In an American Bowl game in Australia in 1999, he was critical of everything Australian. It created such a furor that it even drew the ire of Mike Shanahan. Sharpe vowed not to say another word to the media for the rest of the season and didn't. Sharpe retired before the end of the 2004 season to take a job with CBS-TV to be part of its NFL coverage team.

Rod Smith

Rod Smith is another unknown to make it big. He wasn't even drafted, but he signed as a rookie free agent out of Missouri Southern in 1994.

Smith's debut was every wide receiver's dream. The Broncos and Washington Redskins were tied 31–31 in the third game of the season in 1995. Overtime seemed certain as Elway took the snap for the last play of the regulation at the Washington 43. Elway hurled it to the end zone. Smith found himself one-on-one with All-Pro corner Darrell Green. They both jumped high and wrestled for possession of the ball. Smith came down with it and landed just inside the end zone as the clock ran out. The Broncos had won. That ball is in Smith's trophy case. It was his first catch in the NFL and it went for a touchdown to win a game.

Since his memorable "first catch," Smith has moved to the top of the class as the Broncos most prolific receiver. Smith never quits working to get better, in season or off-season. Going into the 2003 season, he ranked first in receiving yards, first in touchdowns, and second in receptions. His 2000 yardage total of 1,601 receiving yards is Denver's single-one season best.

Smith doesn't appear ready to leave the field and by the time he does he could set very high standards for future generations of players.

The Broncos Were Big around the World

T he Denver Broncos took the game of American football to hundreds of thousands around the world. The NFL started the American Bowl in the 1980s to create new markets for its merchandise. At the time the Broncos were dominating the AFC and appeared in three Super Bowls. John Elway had superstar appeal, so Denver was an obvious team to feature.

The American Bowls were fun. It was preseason, so there wasn't the pressure of a regular season or playoff game, except for the rookies and marginal players trying to make the team. To satisfy the fans the starters played a little more than the usual cameo appearance in preseason. The young players trying to win a job and some veterans resented the long airplane rides and the different food, but every trip was memorable.

Denver met the Los Angeles Rams at London's Wembley Stadium in 1987. Coming a year after The Drive, Elway was known in Great Britain and was a target for the infamous tabloids. The Rams and Broncos gave the 72,786 fans a show, with LA winning 28–27.

There was discussion of canceling the game because of tension between the Arab world and the United States and Great Britain. In April of that year, President Ronald Reagan, with the help of the British, had carried out a bombing raid on Tripoli, Libya, in retaliation for terrorist acts attributed to President Muammar Gaddafi. The decision was made to play the game, but the possibility of terrorism was taken seriously. On arrival the travel party received a briefing from U.S. Embassy officials. Security at the hotel was tight. Scotland Yard detectives rode the buses to and from practice and perimeter security was set up around the practice field at the Crystal Palace Soccer Club. In order to blend in, the detectives wore Bronco coaching outfits. This created a funny incident during an evening reception. The Scotland Yard people had only seen the coaches in their coaching garb and didn't realize that they would change into suits for the reception. They showed up in caps, Bronco shirts, and khaki pants and didn't blend in at all.

Denver's next overseas trip was to Tokyo in the opening preseason game of 1990. The nearly eighteen-hour trip, the stifling heat and humidity in the Japanese capital, and the long trip back took its toll on the team and on Coach Dan Reeves, who suffered a near heart attack when the team returned to its Greeley training camp. After a procedure to clear an artery, Reeves was back on the job quickly.

The Broncos practiced at the Olympic Stadium, and when the buses arrived at Olympic Park the first day, thousands of Japanese kids greeted them and were chanting, "Eh-way, Eh-way, Eh-way." When John appeared the cheers were deafening.

Because of the heat and different culture most of the players didn't venture too far from the hotel. In all of the

Boy, We Really Showed Them

The bus trip to the practice facility was long and tedious through the midday London traffic. I was on a tight schedule to get back to the hotel for a radio program and *Denver Post* columnist Dick Connor was on a tight deadline as well, so we decided we would take the train back to central London, even though the entire party was warned to stay with the security people and ride the buses.

When we arrived at the train station, we realized that we weren't the only ones with the idea. Forsaking the security, several players had quickly changed and were already on the platform. When the train arrived at Victoria Station, none of us had any idea how to get to the hotel, which was located next to Hyde Park. A kindly lady instructed us to catch the Underground to Hyde Park. The players, except for Vance Johnson and Mark Jackson, two of the Amigos (see the next chapter), headed for the Underground. The Amigos said they knew the way by foot, so Connor and I decided to go with them. After 2 blocks it was obvious that they had no idea how to get there. They were out in front of us and left us stranded when they jumped in a taxi. It took us forever to find a taxi and by the time we arrived at the hotel, the buses had just pulled up. Boy, we really showed them how clever we were.

venues, Bronco officials tried to keep the food as American as they could.

The game at the Tokyo Dome was a dull one. Denver beat Seattle, 10–7.

The Broncos were back in Europe in 1992 to play the Miami Dolphins at the famous Olympic Stadium in Berlin.

This American Bowl featured two of the best quarterbacks in the game, Elway and Dan Marino. American football had become popular in Germany, and there were a number of club teams in the Budweiser League. The German players were guests at the daily practices and on occasion got to actually run plays with the Broncos and Dolphins. The teams

practiced on the huge parade ground outside of the stadium, where Hitler had staged rallies in Nazi Germany.

The practices created an international incident of sorts. The area is located in the British sector of Berlin and we all know how protective the British are of their lawns. The military personnel in charge took great pride in that grass. It had rained before the first practice, and when the large vehicles with the film crews rolled out to the field to film practice, they left big ruts in the lawn. The British officers were extremely unhappy and took immediate action. They brought in large sheets of plywood so the vehicles could move up and down the sidelines without damaging the grass.

Perhaps the highlight of the trip was the arrival at the hotel during the noon hour. The Intercontinental Hotel borders the Tierpark, a large wooded area in the middle of the city. As the buses rolled on the street next to the park, the players noticed several *fräuleins* enjoying the warm sun during their lunch break. Not uncommon in Europe, they were sunbathing in the nude. The American football players were wide-eyed. The buses almost tipped over as the passengers jammed one side to look out the windows.

The players adapted well to Germany. They enjoyed the beer halls and the food. The history of Berlin, the fact that the Berlin Wall had just come down, and a tour of historic Potsdam kept their interest.

The Dolphins won the game 31–27.

Two years later, Denver was in Europe once again, this time in Barcelona, Spain, to face the Los Angeles Raiders. The intriguing thing about this matchup was that the two bitter rivals were meeting for the third consecutive game. Denver had blown a big lead to the Raiders in Los Angeles in the final game of the previous season, losing 33–30 in overtime. The two teams knew they would face each other in the wild card game the next week, and the contest would decide who would have the home field. The Broncos had to return to the Los Angeles Coliseum and were eliminated by the Raiders 42–24. Going back to 1992, it was the fourth straight loss to LA Coach Wade Phillips and his staff were still smarting from the way the season ended the year before and didn't hide the fact that even though this was a preseason game, they wanted to win it. They felt that psychologically the Bronco players needed to beat the Raiders.

Coaches say that one practice against a different team in training camp is equal to two practices against your own team, so the normal procedure was that teams practiced against each other for a couple of days as well as playing the game. The Broncos and Raiders refused to practice against each other.

The Broncos went for a day at the beach in Sitges, a resort city south of Barcelona on the Mediterranean Sea. The host was the Barcelona Dragons of NFL Europe, who have their headquarters in Sitges. Many of us walked the streets of the historic town, but the players were intrigued by the fact that many of the women on the beach were topless, again something not uncommon in Europe, but certainly fascinating for American football players.

Two outstanding quarterbacks, Steve Young of the 49ers (left) and John Elway, drew such a crowd at a personal appearance that it stopped traffic in downtown Tokyo. (Courtesy Eric Lars Bakke/Rich Clarkson and Associates)

The game did not go well for the Broncos. The Raiders beat them 25–22 at Olympic Stadium. Los Angeles later extended their streak by winning the two regular season games as well.

Mike Shanahan replaced Phillips as head coach of the Broncos and for the second straight year, the Broncos were headed overseas. This time it was a return visit to Tokyo and a date with the San Francisco 49ers. Shanahan had been the offensive coordinator in San Francisco and came to Denver after the 49ers won the Super Bowl. Ironically, Denver hosted the 'Niners in the first preseason game that year, winning 9–7, then had to go to Japan to meet them again the next week.

Broncos Make a Historical Flight

Denver International Airport had opened in February 1995 and officials hoped that conditions would be right for the Broncos to make a historical flight. They were. The Japan Airlines Boeing 747 took off from Denver and didn't touch down until it was at Tokyo's Narita International Airport. It was the first nonstop flight from Denver's new airport to a Pacific Rim country. The flight took nearly seventeen hours, but everyone felt it was not as tiring as the one a few years before that stopped in Seattle.

The flight was a boon to any movie buffs on board. If you could manage not to sleep, you could have watched seven movies. They kept them going throughout the flight. Several players boasted they saw them all.

Elway was again in the spotlight and this time shared it with Steve Young of the 49ers. The two made an appearance in a brand new NFL store in downtown Tokyo. The crowd was so large that it spilled out into the street for blocks and stopped traffic.

The Broncos made it two straight over the 49ers with a 24–10 win in the Tokyo Dome.

It was Mexico City in 1997. Denver had been upset by Jacksonville in the playoffs to end a 13–3 season prematurely. The Bronco players knew they had a good team, used that defeat as motivation, and took the preseason seriously, hoping to build momentum.

Denver faced the Miami Dolphins before the largest crowd to ever watch the Broncos, as 104,629 jammed Estadio Guillermo Candedo, and there was a *Monday Night Football* audience as well. The festive mood turned sour when Elway came out of the game holding his arm in obvious pain. He had undergone shoulder surgery in the off-season, and even though he had recovered by training camp, Bronco fans had visions of the season going down the drain before it really started. Denver lost 38–19, but concern over Elway overshadowed the game.

Elway was on the field for the first regular season game, however, and the Broncos went on to the Super Bowl championship.

In 1999 the Broncos gave the country a preview of the new Olympic Stadium in Sydney, Australia, which would be used for the Olympics the next year. Denver had a veteran football team that had endured several overseas trips and had just won two straight Super Bowls. Elway had retired, and the long trip halfway around the world was not popular with his former teammates.

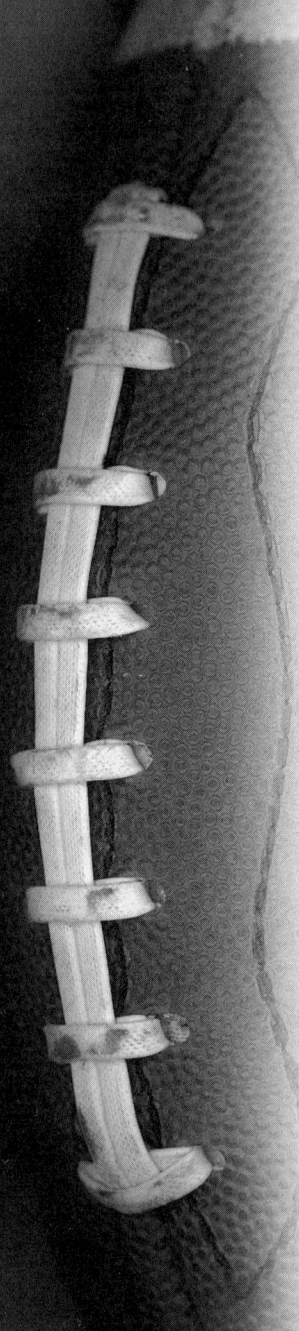

Never Doubt the Greek

Head trainer Steve "The Greek" Antonopolus and his assistants huddled around the grimacing Elway on the sidelines. An anxious Shanahan awaited the verdict, but it was apparent Elway was finished for the night. The diagnosis was a rupture in a tendon in the right biceps. It was obviously painful and sounded serious. Shanahan and Antonopolus answered the postgame questions as best they could. The Greek said that he didn't feel it was a season-ending injury. Antonopolus was quite optimistic, saying that in his opinion when the pain subsided, Elway would be fine, that he could play without that tendon.

The media didn't buy it, which added to the consternation of the fans. On the talk shows everybody was a medical expert. The newspapers gave the public a lesson in anatomy with graphic illustrations of the injury. Some even predicted that Elway's career was over. Antonopolus held to his opinion and proclaimed that the media hysteria was a bunch of nonsense. While the Broncos didn't rush things, Elway started some light throwing within a week and as predicted by Antonopolus, when the pain subsided, he didn't seem to be disabled.

Elway opened the season at quarterback against the Chiefs at Mile High, and as if to prove he was okay, he connected with Rod Smith on a pass that traveled more than 50 yards in the air.

Tight end Shannon Sharpe let it get to him and in his own colorful way, created a bit of an international incident by loudly criticizing the weather, the beer, the pubs, the time difference, the television shows, and anything else he could think of. Sharpe had been passed by while waiting for a taxi and charged racism. Because of the outburst that was widely reported in Australia and the United States, Sharpe came under criticism himself, by the owner, the coach, and the media. He decided not to open his mouth the rest of the season (a difficult task), and he held to it.

The Broncos beat the Chargers 20–17 and happily headed home.

Cookie, Lyle, the Amigos, and Others

There are the great and the near great, and then there are the players one will never forget because, well, they were characters. But they were good players too.

Cookie Gilchrist

We'll start with Cookie Gilchrist, who had two stints with Denver, one in 1965 and another in 1967. The Broncos acquired the big running back from Buffalo, but Gilchrist balked at leaving the East. He complained about his contract offer, and while threatening to retire, he came to Denver and set up headquarters in a downtown hotel. Meanwhile, his future teammates were at training camp. After about a week, Gilchrist came out of hiding and had a change of heart. He decided he liked Denver, so he'd accept the trade and report. He said he would not only play, but he would bring the Broncos a championship. But he insisted on some incentives in his contract, one of which would create a problem late in the season.

Cookie became Denver's first professional sports celebrity. He drove around town in a gold Cadillac with a message painted on the side: "Lookie, lookie, here comes Cookie." The fans loved him and loved his stories. He was a fixture at civic club luncheons and the Quarterback Club. He gained 954

Running back Cookie Gilchrist was Denver's first pro football celebrity.
(Courtesy Rich Clarkson and Associates)

yards that earned him a $5,000 bonus. Like most things with Gilchrist, that bonus didn't come without controversy. His contract called for the bonus if he gained 900 yards. He hadn't reached that number by the final game. The team was headed to Kansas City, but Cookie refused to fly on the charter. He called the plane "rickety" and accused management of being cheap. He said he wouldn't play in the final game. But then he thought about that $5,000 and took a commercial flight. Management had every right to suspend him, but sensitive to the criticism that they were a cheap organization, they allowed him to play, despite Coach Max Speedie's objections.

The next year, Speedie and Gilchrist battled during training camp, Cookie left and said he would sit out the season.

I'll Take Him

When it became apparent that Cookie Gilchrist's playing days were over, the Broncos placed him on waivers. Any team in the league could claim him for $100. A female Bronco fan misinterpreted the newspaper story on the subject.

Al King, the Broncos' director of public relations, took the phone call from the lady. She asked if anyone could claim Cookie for $100?

King answered, "Yes."

She said, "I'll do it."

Confused, King said, "Do what?"

She answered, "Claim Cookie. How do I make out the check?"

King had to straighten out her misconception, explaining only "teams" could claim him. They didn't ask Cookie; he might have liked the idea.

"Lookie, lookie, there goes Cookie." He was traded to Miami.

"Lookie, lookie, here comes Cookie," again. One of Lou Saban's first moves when he was named coach in 1967 was to bring Gilchrist back. Cookie had helped Saban's Bills win a title and they were great friends. Gilchrist broke his leg in the opening game of the season. He never played again.

Lyle Alzado

He wore number 77 and in a television special we were doing on the Broncos' first twenty years, he announced to the camera, "I'm mean and I'm tough and I'm the best defensive end the Broncos have ever seen . . . ME . . . Lyle Alzado."

Alzado was a bear of a man with a heart of gold. Beneath his rough, tough exterior was an intelligent, sensitive man. Alzado got his degree in special education and worked with handicapped children. In 1977 he received the Byron (Whizzer) White Man of the Year Award from the NFL Players Association. The countless hours and the money he spent in charitable pursuits while in Denver, unfortunately, largely went unnoticed.

He was drafted by the Broncos from Yankton College in 1971. Don't let that South Dakota education throw you. Alzado was street-smart and a tough kid who grew up in Brooklyn, New York. Lyle could never decide whether he was more Italian or more Jewish.

Broncos assistant coach Stan Jones was responsible for bringing Alzado to Denver, and it was by accident. Jones had car trouble while driving through Montana and to kill time while his vehicle was being repaired in Butte, he went to Montana Tech to look at some film. He watched the Copper Bowl where Tech had played Yankton College.

Jones said, "I saw this one kid from Yankton, number 77, making all the tackles. The coach was new and had no idea who he was. We located a program and learned that his name was Lyle Alzado. I turned his name into the coach covering the Dakotas, Whitey Dovell, and he liked him. We got some film on him, so we drafted him."

Alzado had a fierce desire to win and became an important part of the Orange Crush. But it wasn't always easy. As Defensive Coordinator Joe Collier remembered, "He was a tough guy to coach. We found out we couldn't yell at him in practice because he would pout and get mad and walk off the practice field. He'd come back the next day and apologize. Once we learned how to deal with him, it got better. He wasn't a great practice player, but once the game started on Sunday, he gave you everything he had."

In the summer of 1979, while Alzado was in a contract stalemate with General Manager Fred Gehrke, some local promoters convinced him to get into the boxing ring for an exhibition bout with the retired heavyweight champion, Muhammad Ali. Alzado could box. He was a Golden Gloves regional champion and had twenty-seven straight victories. In Alzado's competitive mind, this was more than an exhibition. He was going to take on Ali.

It was the big news of a routine summer. The bout was on a Saturday afternoon, outdoors, at Mile High Stadium. The public was gobbling up the tickets. To promote the event, a ring was set up in the Skyline Plaza in downtown Denver, so fans could watch Alzado spar. I was the ring announcer and

Defensive end Lyle Alzado was a man about town in Denver, but he also did a lot of charity work in the community. (Courtesy Rich Clarkson and Associates)

We've Got a Problem, Son

Lyle Alzado could never seem to stay out of the spotlight. It was always something he said, or something he wore on the nightclub circuit, or some bizarre activity that added to his celebrity. He also had a knack for falling in love.

His position coach, Stan Jones, remembers getting a call in the middle of the night from Lyle announcing that he was in love.

Jones told him, "So what else is new. You wake me up in the middle of the night to tell me you're in love?"

"But you don't understand, coach. She's married."

"Well, Lyle, you ought to know better than that, but I don't see that it's a problem for the team."

"Yes it is, coach; she's married to one of my teammates."

"We've got a problem, son."

Red Miller, who bought into the whole thing, refereed the sparring session.

Another major media event was the weigh-in in the ballroom of a downtown hotel. It was made to order for Ali, who took charge of the proceedings and orchestrated the affair. I was standing next to Alzado and Ali, and I heard the champ's instructions to Lyle to play along with him and they would have a pushing and shoving match. At Ali's instigation they were soon yelling at each other, shoving each other, and creating chaos. Uniformed police rushed to keep them apart. This wasn't part of the act and the promoters were taken by surprise. Ali was escorted off the stage and was yelling at

Alzado, "This ain't an exhibition any more tough guy. I'm coming after you. You'd better be ready." For Ali it was part of his act, but Alzado took it seriously. He got that fierce look in his eyes and screamed back at the champ, "I'm going to take you apart."

The scene at Mile High was like out of the 1920s—a heavyweight fight in a big stadium. In the first round, Ali did it all. We saw the Rope a Dope. Ali floated like a butterfly and stung like a bee. He took some of the zing off of his punches but landed some solid blows to show one and all that he could end this whenever he wanted. Ali toyed with Alzado for the remaining five rounds and even feigned pain when Lyle landed a good punch.

When it was over, Alzado deluded himself into believing that he could make it in the heavyweight ranks. He gave Gehrke an ultimatum to meet his contract demands, or he would quit football and pursue the heavyweight championship. Gehrke's answer was to trade him to Cleveland.

It was like sending him to Siberia. He had no audience and his performance suffered. His exile ended when the Browns sent him to the Los Angeles Raiders. In the glare of Hollywood, Alzado flourished on and off the field. He even started an acting career.

The story doesn't have a happy ending though. In his pursuit of excellence, Lyle used a lot of body-building drugs, many that were harmful, but at that time not enough was known about their effects on the body. Lyle developed a rare form of cancer and devoted the rest of his life to telling his story. He appeared on most of the talk shows and warned young people to stay away from drugs.

The last time I visited with Lyle was on the Raiders bench in 1991. He was a shadow of his former self. He was wearing a

Lyle Alzado (right) fought an exhibition bout with Muhammad Ali. Here he prepares for a public sparring session in downtown Denver. Larry Zimmer (left) interviews Broncos Coach Red Miller, who was the referee. (Courtesy Larry Zimmer's personal collection)

bandana to cover the chemotherapy-caused baldness. He still had that look in his eyes when he told me, "I'm going to beat this thing."

He lost that final battle. He was dead in May 1992, at the age of 42.

The Three Amigos

The Broncos were the most successful team of the second half of the decade of the 1980s with three AFC championships. Because of his comebacks, his style of play, and his love of movie hero John Wayne, Elway was labeled the "Gunslinger." Posters around town of John in cowboy costume and two six guns were bestsellers. Joining him in the spotlight were "The Three Amigos": Vance Johnson, Mark Jackson, and Ricky Nattiel, small, but fleet receivers. They looked like bugs running around the field. An injury to veteran Steve Watson in 1987 opened the door for the Amigos to shine.

They might have been small, but they made big plays. Jackson had caught the touchdown pass that climaxed The Drive in Cleveland, and he was a rookie.

The three hung out together and were the best of friends. Nattiel was the quiet one; Jackson was the happy-go-lucky one, always with a big smile; Johnson was the flamboyant one, who drove fast cars, lived in a big house and sported outlandish haircuts. Jackson and Johnson were regulars at Denver's night-clubs and strip joints, but Jackson kept his nose clean.

Johnson promoted himself as "The Vance." He was a nice guy, an extrovert, and loved to be in the spotlight. Johnson said that he really had a dual personality. The nice guy and "The Vance." He admits that "The Vance" often took hold of him and caused him to ignore responsibilities.

When he signed his pro contract, he instantly had more money than he had ever known and he spent it. The football hero also had all the women he wanted. It cost him two marriages. The abuse of his wives and his girlfriends ultimately became public knowledge and ruined his image. He once did some jail time for domestic violence.

But Johnson also had an artistic side. He was a fine artist and would spend his free moments at training camp sketching, particularly the faces of women. He said he did it for himself and never tried to sell his paintings, but they did bring in a lot of bucks at charity auctions in Denver.

Vance was an outstanding athlete. Aside from his football feats at Arizona, he also won the NCAA long jump championship in 1983. He combined his athletic ability and his artistry into dancing and once appeared on stage with the Colorado Ballet.

The nice guy that sketched and danced ultimately got control of his life and after years of counseling, Johnson straightened himself out. He became a successful businessman, owning and operating a mortgage loan business in Grand Junction, Colorado. Ironically, Mark Jackson is in the same business but with a competing company also in Grand Junction.

The Three Amigos reached their zenith during the playoffs and Super Bowl after the 1987 season. There was a video and posters, and they enjoyed the attention. Nattiel had a touchdown catch in the early minutes of Super Bowl XXII against the Redskins in 1988, but Jackson and Johnson were quiet.

Nattiel was released by the Broncos in 1992. Jackson got a big contract with the New York Giants, and Johnson was traded to the Vikings. Before the 1993 season was over, he came back to the Broncos but broke his leg. After recovering,

The Famous Poster

The famous poster that sold more than 150,000 copies featured the Amigos in football pants, bare chests, shoulder pads, and sombreros. It had a WANTED sign on it and was entitled, "Adios Amigos."

Johnson put up his own money to produce the poster and wanted to call it, "The Good, the Bad, and the Ugly." He explained the reason in his book, *The Vance.*

"Since Mark was perceived as a good guy, I was perceived as the hell-raiser, and Ricky was so ugly, we thought it would be a good title. Ricky wouldn't go for it."

The three ultimately had to file a suit against their business manager over proceeds from the poster. It was settled out of court, but Johnson said they were really cheated out of a lot of money and the settlement didn't cover it.

he spent some time with the Chargers and finished his career in Denver in 1995.

Bill Romanowski

Bill Romanowski was a player who led by enthusiasm and was a key defensive leader in the Broncos' Super Bowl championship years. Mike Shanahan brought Romanowski to Denver because he was playoff hardened, having been in the playoffs six of the eight years at San Francisco and Philadelphia before coming to Denver. He had played in five NFC title games and two Super Bowls.

Growing up in Vernon, Connecticut, he was an all-sports participant and dreamed of playing professional basketball. His success on the football field in high school made him change his mind.

Romanowski was a favorite of the media. The television reporters sought him out in the locker room. He always had a comment and sometimes it wasn't kind to his teammates or the opponents. On the field he was in another world mentally. His teammate, John Mobley, said he's like Jekyll and Hyde, mean in a game, one of the nicest guys away from the field.

In a 1997 preseason game against Carolina, Romanowski drew criticism for ending quarterback Kerry Collins's season with a helmet-first hit that broke Collins's jaw.

Romo was rarely injured, and if he was, he didn't let on. He was on the field every game. He took pride in his body and was a frequent visitor to the weight room. He said, "I try to keep myself in top condition all the time, whether it's eating right, getting massages, working out, whatever."

Romanowski's wife, Julie, was also into bodybuilding and the two, scantily clad, were featured in a story with a full-page picture in the *Sports Illustrated* swimsuit edition. Romanowski took a lot of pills—vitamins and various supplements. Even under scrutiny, it was never found that he took illegal drugs. Romanowski's popularity in Denver eventually waned and he opted out, signing as a free agent with the Oakland Raiders in 2002.

Bill Romanowski was a favorite of the media. (Courtesy Eric Lars Bakke/Rich Clarkson and Associates)

It Could Have Torn the Team Apart

Bill Romanowski's enthusiasm got him in trouble in a game late in the 1997 season. The Broncos had opened 11–2 and had a playoff position clinched, but they had not clinched the division title and home field advantage. They had blown a 21–7 lead and lost in Pittsburgh the week before and were playing the 49ers in San Francisco on Monday Night Football. The game was not going well and the team was frustrated about the possibility of losing its second in a row.

For whatever reason, after a tackle on wide receiver J. J. Stokes, Romo spit in his face. The ABC cameras captured it and reran it time after time. The national media and the 49ers weren't the only ones who were outraged. Many of Romanowski's own teammates were openly critical. The next day a humble Romanowski begged forgiveness in a team meeting. Elway says everyone understood the intensity with which Romo played the game, and they were willing to grant forgiveness.

What could have torn the team apart seemed to bring it together. Denver won the final game the next week and didn't stop winning until they took the Super Bowl.

Darren Drozdov

Who? Well, this chapter wouldn't be complete without the mention of the little-known defensive lineman who had only a brief career with Denver. Darren Drozdov was a nose tackle and thus played right over the ball. Why is he notable? Well, he had a nervous stomach and before the play started he would get so excited that he would vomit on the ball. Trust me.

Mile High Becomes a Parking Lot: Broncomania Remains

A ticket to a Denver Bronco game continues to be the hottest ticket in town. Going through the 2003 campaign, every home game has been sold out since the beginning of the 1970 season, with the exception of the two replacement games played during the strike in 1987. Both games were sold out before the strike.

This love affair with the football team started before the Broncos had recorded a winning season.

Broncomania took hold in 1977 when, under Red Miller, the Broncos were 12–2, went to the playoffs for the first time, and then to the Super Bowl. Miller had urged the fans to turn Mile High Stadium into a hostile environment for the visiting team, and the fans obliged. In game five of that season, the Broncos beat the Raiders in Oakland 30–7 and more than 10,000 fans jammed Stapleton International Airport to greet the team charter. The airplane was brought into a gate on the smaller "A" Concourse where the police could gain a measure

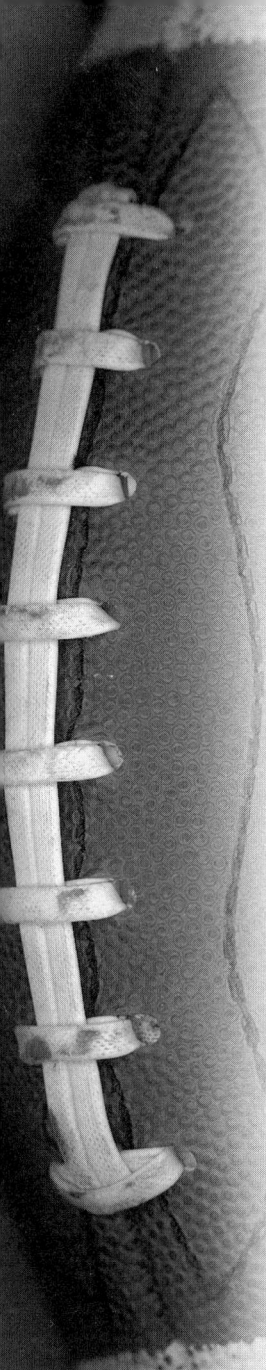

"Big Orange—How Sweet It Is"

Mayor Bill McNichols was often referred to as "The Broncos Number One Fan." Even the mayor knew that he was number two. Number one was Charlie Goldberg, a long-time Denver businessman and political leader. His pastime was the Broncos. Goldberg made a significant contribution to Denver and to the Broncos. He even received mail addressed to "Charlie Bronco."

Goldberg acquired the Barnett Company, which was the holder of several diverse businesses, but primarily was a wrecking company. Goldberg worked hard and became a wealthy man, but he was always modest. He lived well into his 90s and never missed a Broncos home game.

He founded the Bronco Quarterback Club and The Active Roster (a group of business people who help players make the transition from football to the business world), and he built the Mile High Stadium Club.

Goldberg's dream was to turn Mile High Stadium into a "sea of orange" and even copyrighted the slogan "Big Orange—How Sweet It Is." He hatched the idea of Orange Monday when Denver played its first Monday Night Football game in 1973. He was a major backer of Mayor Bill and he went to him with the idea. McNichols was cool to it because of the color orange, which, for an Irish Catholic, was politically incorrect. When the mayor turned him down by saying, "I'm Irish," an indignant Goldberg retorted, "Well, I'm Jewish and what does that have to do with anything." Orange Monday became a reality.

of control by creating a lane for the players to walk through. Fans were screaming, crying, throwing beer, and pushing others out of the way to touch one of their returning heroes. The crowds at the airport became commonplace after every road win that season, and the Denver Police Department's budget was being taxed because of the overtime pay. When asked about that problem, Mayor Bill McNichols, a huge Bronco fan, chomped down on his cigar and smiled broadly. Hizzoner said, "How can I worry about that when we have another big game next week?"

More and more fans began wearing the team colors. Men and women dyed their hair and painted their skin orange. Orange cars were being driven around town and more than one homeowner painted his home orange. Some city buses were painted orange. Sales of the drink, Orange Crush, reached new highs. The Barrel Man—wearing his oversized Orange Crush can—was as popular as the players. At least one person had his dog dyed orange. As the first playoff game in Bronco history approached, against Pittsburgh on Christmas Eve, people were buying orange Christmas trees and giving orange toilet seats as gifts. Local stores sold out of Bronco merchandise on a daily basis. Jon Keyworth's song "Make Those Miracles Happen" was a best-seller. One radio station promised game tickets to the person who performed the most outrageous stunt. The winner ran naked through downtown.

Broncomania never really reached those extremes again. After all, that was the first time. But it hasn't really waned all that much either. For one thing it got more sophisticated. The Barrel Man was an unofficial mascot. The official mascot became "Miles," who not only appears at home games but at events in the city. The team is also represented by Thunder, a purebred Arabian stallion, who circles the field after every

Denver's famed "Barrel Man" is in the fan section of the Pro Football Hall of Fame in Canton, Ohio. What did he wear under the barrel?
(Courtesy Eric Lars Bakke/Rich Clarkson and Associates)

What Did the Barrel Man Wear under the Barrel?

The Barrel Man came about because of a bet. Tim McKernan was a big Bronco fan and always led cheers in his section. He created an Orange Crush can out of a barrel and his brother bet him he wouldn't wear it to a game. Actually, the bet was that Tim would wear only the barrel. McKernan won't let on if that's all he wore.

It started a tradition. McKernan, a now retired mechanic for United Airlines, wore suspenders to hold up the barrel, an orange cowboy hat, and orange cowboy boots. He was there even in the coldest weather.

The Barrel Man is so much a part of Bronco history, that McKernan has been inducted into the special fan wing of the Pro Football Hall of Fame.

Denver score. Another fixture is the Bronco Cheerleaders, whose members are selected through auditions held each spring. They are known for their distinctive western uniforms.

The Bronco Cheerleaders had some predecessors. The first group was the Bronkettes, a dance team of little girls. The South Stands had its own cheerleaders for a while. The next major group was the Bronco Belles, which evolved into the Pony Express. They had great outfits and were an accomplished dance team, but when some of the girls took off their outfits for *Playboy* magazine, the group was disbanded. For seventeen years the Broncos had no cheerleaders, until the present group was organized in 1993.

Another Bronco fixture at early games was the Bronco Band, a seventeen-piece group, conducted by Jess Girardi. They had distinctive uniforms, featuring blue blazers. Girardi was a high school music teacher and band director and planned halftime shows, bringing some of the top high school and college bands into Mile High Stadium. The Bronco Band was disbanded in the early 1990s as the marketing staff moved to a more contemporary rock style on the public address system.

The team uniforms also became more contemporary in 1997. When the uniform models were unveiled, the reviews were not good. The light blue was changed to navy blue. The home jerseys would be navy blue with orange and white trim, and the helmet went to the navy blue with a new, more contemporary, logo. Orange had been so important to the Bronco past, fans were upset. In an attempt at damage control, owner Pat Bowlen proclaimed that the uniforms were "predominantly orange," even though they featured only orange stripes. The dispute was soon forgotten when the 1997 Broncos, in the new unis, started winning games and won the Super Bowl.

Another major change was the replacement of venerable Mile High Stadium. Major League Baseball's Colorado Rockies had moved into brand new Coors Field in 1995. The Pepsi Center, a new basketball and hockey arena, was under construction, and Mile High was showing its age. Bowlen felt he needed a new stadium for the Broncos to remain competitive. He, rather than the city, would control the building, and it would have more luxury suites and club seating.

While he never said it, there was a hint in Bowlen's remarks that without a new stadium, the Broncos might not be viable in Denver. NFL Commissioner Paul Tagliabue was more direct when he said that he felt the Broncos couldn't remain in Denver without a new stadium. The populace was split. A segment of the voters were solidly behind the construction of a stadium. Many others were against public money being used to build a new football palace that would be operated by Bowlen. They called it "corporate welfare." There was a third group that hated to give up on Mile High and supported remodeling the old stadium instead of building an entirely new one.

As he had done in the past, businessman Charlie Goldberg took charge of the drive for a new stadium. A group called CFANS (Citizens For A New Stadium) organized the campaign to get the issue on a ballot in the six-county Stadium District. The group made sure the timing of the election was right and ran an efficient campaign. They couldn't have planned it better. The Broncos won the Super Bowl in 1997 and at election time in November 1998 were undefeated. The issue was passed in a landslide vote.

The first landmark to go to pave the way for the new stadium was McNichols Sports Arena. The Nuggets and Avalanche had moved to the Pepsi Center and the space was needed for parking. Progress of the construction of the new stadium, located just south of Mile High, could be charted while watching the Broncos play.

While accepting the new stadium, the fans weren't willing to give up on the name. The newspapers and the talk shows fueled the debate. The Stadium District managers had vowed to help pay part of the construction debt by selling the name. The citizens felt their tax money was going into the construction and they should have a voice, and they wanted to keep the name, Mile High Stadium. Mayor Wellington Webb weighed in on the side of keeping the old name. Public hearings were held, but in the end the name was sold to the mutual fund company, Invesco. In somewhat of a compromise, the official name of the stadium is Invesco Field at Mile High. The *Denver Post* had supported keeping the name Mile High Stadium, and even after the stadium was officially named, mandated that in the paper it would be called "The New Mile High Stadium." This mandate was quietly dropped, and the *Post* now prints the official name.

Mayor Webb also went to battle with the Stadium District on the demolition of the old stadium, which was supposed to start in February 2001. The Webb administration had been stung by delays that stretched on for more than a year in the opening of Denver International Airport, so Webb refused to let the demolition of Mile High start until the new stadium was ready to use. He'd had nightmares of the stadium not being ready, and Broncos games having to be played at the University of Colorado stadium in Boulder or the Air Force Academy stadium in Colorado Springs. Invesco Field opened on time, with the first games played in August 2001. The two stadiums sat side by side for a while, and it was a sad sight to view the tired old lady next to the sparkling new arena.

When Bob Howsam bought the Denver Bears, they were playing in Merchant's Park, which he described as "a wooden termite haven and fire trap." Howsam, with his father and brother, sold $250,000 of personal bonds and borrowed $90,000 to build a new stadium. A mayoral election was in progress and the incumbent, Ben Stapleton, told Howsam he could have the old city dump for $1.00 just to get it cleaned up. Stapleton lost the election to the legendary Quig Newton, who quickly upped the purchase price for the dump to $32,000. Howsam fretted, "That election cost me $31,999."

The new Bears Stadium opened on August 14, 1948. The seating capacity was just over 18,000.

Howsam became involved in the formation of the Continental Baseball League, planned to be a third major league. He financed the construction of stands in right field to add another 8,100 seats, which brought the stadium to major league baseball standards. These would later become the Broncos' famous South Stands. While the Continental League never got off the ground, the American Football League did, and Howsam added portable stands for football on the east side of the stadium, increasing the capacity to 34,657 when the Broncos started play in 1960.

Bears Stadium was now a major league facility but not big enough for the demands of the National Football League after the announced merger with the AFL in 1966. Either a new stadium would have to be built or Bears Stadium enlarged. Gerald Phipps, who had saved the Broncos for Denver in 1965, was the majority owner. He used his political clout to get a Metropolitan Stadium District created. The same legislation called for a bond issue to build a new $20 million stadium near Stapleton International Airport. The voters delivered a crushing blow by turning down the stadium bond issue by a two-to-one margin. Considering the popularity of the football team, to this day no one can really explain this shocking turn of events.

Phipps was keenly disappointed. The pro football merger agreement required 50,000 seats, and the Broncos had only 34,000. Rumors were rampant that Commissioner Pete Rozelle and the NFL owners favored relocating the franchise to Birmingham, Alabama. A number of volunteer groups were formed to help keep the team in Denver. They merged into one organization called "the DOERS"—Denver Organization to Erect the Right Kind of Stadium. Since a new stadium was out, the effort was to build an addition on Bears Stadium. The group had organized collections at civic clubs, in schools, and on street corners. Charlie Goldberg realized that the effort would never succeed. He took over the campaign and got commitments from the business community. The plan was to raise $1.8 million, buy Bears Stadium from Phipps, and give it to the City and County of Denver, which would then pay for adding 16,000 seats by issuing revenue bonds. The campaign was successful. A deck was added to the west side and the capacity was 50,000 when the 1968 season kicked off. On December 14, 1968, the name of the stadium officially became Mile High Stadium.

The sellouts that started in 1970 produced a long waiting list for tickets and dictated another stadium expansion. Again Goldberg headed up the committee as another bond issue went before the voters. It was a close vote this time, but the measure was narrowly approved. It called for new double-decked stands on the east side and on the north end. The capacity would be increased to 75,000. Baseball had to be accommodated, because the Bears still played there, so a revolutionary plan was conceived to move the East Stands in for football and out for baseball.

The Eighth Wonder of the World

There were those who doubted that the engineering feat of moving a structure weighing nine million pounds and standing thirteen stories high on runways of water could be accomplished. There were 90,000 square feet of runways that were flooded, so that the structure literally floated on a .003-inch sheet of water. Hydraulic rams pushed the stands a distance of 145 feet at the rate of 3 feet per second.

The Denver media had dire predictions. Many were making bets as to whether the stands would move or not. "Moving Day" arrived. The engineers were confident. The public was skeptical. The politicians were hopeful. Like the launching of a ship, Mayor McNichols broke a bottle of champagne on the structure, the runways were flooded, and the switch was thrown. Slowly but surely, the stands began to move. There were cheers and sighs of relief. Two hours later, the stands locked in the "back" position.

As a result of the moveable stands, the Bears continued to share the stadium with the Broncos, it provided a field for Denver's major league soccer entry, and for two years it was the home to Major League Baseball's Colorado Rockies, who played at Mile High while awaiting the opening of their new home, Coors Field.

The expanded stadium was ready for the Broncos' 1977 Super Bowl run.

Denver Mayor Bill McNichols christens the "launching" of the new East Stands at Mile High Stadium in 1977. (Courtesy Joe Ciancio Jr.)

Denver's new Invesco Field at Mile High (right) opened for the 2001 season. Mile High Stadium still stood, but it was eventually torn down and replaced with a parking lot. (Courtesy Jamie Schwaberow/Rich Clarkson and Associates)

Mile High Stadium had one more expansion when the Penthouse Suites, housing sixty luxury suites, were built above the west stands.

Mile High was torn down after the 2001 season and the area is now a parking lot. The only part of the stadium that still remains is the twenty-seven-foot high white stallion—Buck the Bronco—that was refurbished and placed above the scoreboard on the south end of Invesco Field.

Today, as I stand in the parking lot north of Invesco Field at Mile High, at a spot that would be in the center of the old gridiron, I close my eyes and can hear the roar of the crowd and the stomping of the feet, and I dream of days gone forever.

The Denver Broncos Ring of Fame

V isitors to Invesco Field at Mile High immediately notice names on the façade of the first deck. This is the Denver Broncos Ring of Fame.

Created in 1984 by Pat Bowlen shortly after he purchased the team, the Ring currently has eighteen members. Bowlen wanted to honor players and administrators who played a major role in the history of the franchise and establish a link with the colorful history of the team.

A player must be retired for five years before becoming eligible for election. Bowlen set up a four-man committee to consider the candidates—a member of the print media, a member of the electronic media, a representative of the fans, and Bowlen. It takes a unanimous vote to elect someone to the Ring of Fame.

The first committee, along with Bowlen, consisted of sports columnist Dick Connor, broadcaster Bob Martin, and legendary fan Charlie Goldberg.

The original class, in 1984, took in players from the early years—running back Floyd Little, wide receiver Lionel Taylor, defensive end Rich Jackson, and safety Austin "Goose" Gonsoulin. The following year, the committee honored former owner Gerald Phipps, who saved the franchise on at least three occasions. Quarterbacks Frank Tripucka and

John Elway's induction in the Broncos Ring of Fame on opening night of the 1999 season. His wife, Janet, and his four children joined him on the field for the ceremony. The children from left to right are Jack, Jordan, Juliana, and Jessica. (Courtesy Jamie Schwaberow/Rich Clarkson and Associates)

Charley Johnson, along with defensive tackle Paul Smith, were selected in 1986; safety Billy Thompson in 1987; quarterback Craig Morton and wide receiver Haven Moses (the M and M Connection), along with placekicker Jim Turner in 1988; and linebacker Randy Gradishar in 1989.

Until 1989 there had been an inductee each year, but it wasn't until 1992 that the next member was inducted. Bowlen felt that the committee had sufficiently honored the past and started to look to players who played under his ownership. The makeup of the committee also changed because of the deaths

Pat Bowlen— A Model Owner

Gerald Phipps is the only nonplayer whose name appears on the Broncos Ring of Fame. He saved the Broncos in the 1960s and made them a winning team in the 1970s.

After the short tenure of Edgar Kaiser, Pat Bowlen purchased the franchise in 1984, and as president and CEO, has presided over two decades of success—back-to-back Super Bowl championships, five AFC championships, and ten playoff seasons. Bowlen is a recognized civic leader and gives back to the community through Bronco Charities. He is an energetic hands-on owner, who is smart enough to let the football people run the football operation.

He has also provided leadership in the NFL and played a key role in the league's labor and television contracts. He is the chairman of the Broadcasting Committee and a key member of the Management Council Executive Committee. He was instrumental in bringing to the NFL the most lucrative single-sport television contract in history, worth $18 billion.

Longtime NFL executive Val Pinchbeck, who represented the league office in the television negotiations, said of Bowlen, "He has a real strong sense of what should happen. He got to know the network executives over a period of time and retains a good relationship with them. This is good for the league."

of Martin and Connor. I became the representative of the electronics media and columnist Woody Paige replaced Connor, only to resign after a couple of years. Bowlen abandoned his original idea for media committee members, and asked former defensive coordinator Joe Collier to join the committee. When Goldberg died, former general manager John Beake became the fourth member.

Every fan and sportswriter has a favorite Bronco they feel should be on the Ring, and the selection committee is bombarded with suggestions and criticized for not electing certain former players.

Linebacker Tom Jackson was selected in 1992, followed by corner back Louis Wright in 1993. There were no additions until quarterback John Elway in 1999. The committee waived the five-year rule for Elway, who entered the Ring the year after his retirement. The most recent two members were inducted in 2001—safety Dennis Smith and linebacker Karl Mecklenburg.

Along with the Ring of Fame, Bowlen also wanted to link to the past and honor it by inviting back all former players for the Annual Alumni Weekend. A lavish dinner, a golf tournament, and introductions at the Sunday game are all part of the weekend. This is when new inductees are honored, but Alumni Weekend is held even if there isn't a new name on the Ring.

From the Snow Bowl to the Super Bowl: the Broncos' Most Memorable Games

Every football team has memorable games. Some you remember because of the significance. Some you remember because of an individual performance. Some you remember because it simply was a great game. I've tried to make this list reasonable, and I realize that my list will probably be different from ones compiled by other Broncos fans.

Super Bowl XXXII—Broncos 31, Packers 24
(January 25, 1998—San Diego)

Super Bowl XXXII would have to top any list of memorable Bronco games. It was Denver's first Super Bowl win after four losses. The Broncos were playing the defending champion Green Bay Packers and were a decided underdog. The Packers started by making the predictions look good. A Brett Favre pass to Antonio Freeman put Green Bay in front, but Denver came right back with a touchdown run from Terrell Davis. John

Terrell Davis scores one of his three touchdowns against Green Bay in Super Bowl XXXII. (Courtesy Rich Clarkson/Rich Clarkson and Associates)

Elway scored on a short run and Jason Elam kicked a 51-yard field goal and Denver led 17–7 in the second quarter. The Broncos never again trailed, even though the Packers tied it at 17 and 24. The Broncos stopped two fourth period drives and scored what proved to be the winning touchdown on a 1-yard run by Davis, his third TD of the game. Green Bay got the ball back with 1:45 remaining and indeed did move into Denver territory, but the Bronco defense held and the final score was 31–24.

Super Bowl XXXIII–Broncos 34, Falcons 19
(January 31, 1999–Miami)

This game was John Elway's swan song and he was superb. He passed for 336 yards, had an 80-yard touchdown pass to Rod Smith, and scored a touchdown himself. He was selected the game's most valuable player. A 32-yard field goal by Morton Anderson put Atlanta ahead in the first quarter, but Denver outscored the Falcons 31–3 over the next forty-four minutes and had an insurmountable 31–6 lead entering the fourth quarter, winning the game 34–19. Davis ran for 105 yards, setting an NFL record with his seventh straight 100-yard game in the postseason.

The Drive–Broncos 23, Browns 20
(January 11, 1987–Cleveland)

This was John Elway's coming of age as he engineered a 98-yard, 15 play drive in the final 5:43 of the game. His 5-yard touchdown pass to Mark Jackson with 0:57 left put Denver in position to tie the game. Rich Karlis tied it and sent it into overtime. Cleveland had the first possession in overtime, but the Broncos stopped them. Elway hit big passes to John Mobley and Steve Watson and got the ball to the Brown 15 yard line. Karlis nailed a 33-yard field goal to win the game.

The Drive, Part II–Broncos 26, Oilers 24
(January 4, 1992–Mile High Stadium)

After reaching the Super Bowl in three of four years in the late 1980s, Denver had a tough season in 1990, but in 1991 the Broncos were back in the playoffs against the powerful "run-and-shoot" offense of the Houston Oilers. Elway says this is his favorite comeback. Quarterback Warren Moon had the Oilers ahead 14–0 five minutes into the contest.

It was 21–6 before the Denver defense began to solve the Houston patterns.

Elway went to work and the Broncos narrowed the gap to one point late in the game. With the clock nearing the two-minute warning, the Bronco defense stopped the Oilers but used all of its time-outs to conserve the clock. Punter Greg Montgomery seemed to seal Denver's fate with a boot that went dead at the 2 yard line. But wait a minute. Remember Cleveland in 1986? The Drive? Once again, the Broncos had them where they wanted them.

Elway recalls: "I remember running on the field thinking that here we are on the 2 yard line again. Just like in Cleveland in 1986. But this was a different situation. We needed just a field goal, not a touchdown. In Cleveland we had five or six minutes and we had time-outs. Now we had two minutes and no time outs. The clock was much more of a factor."

Elway's first pass went for 22 yards, but three plays later he faced fourth and 6 at the Denver 28. Elway looked over the field, was flushed out of the pocket, tucked the ball under his arm, and took off for the sidelines and the first-down marker. He made it with a yard to spare before going out at the 35. Three incompleted passes later and the ball was in the same spot with 0:59 showing on the clock: fourth and 10.

Elway said, "They thought I might run again, so this time they didn't stay back. The cornerback came off Vance [Johnson] to stop the run. Vance was open, but I had to loft the ball over the top. That may have been one of the worst passes I've ever thrown. It was wobbly, but fortunately it got there."

Denver had the ball at Houston's 21 after a 44-yard gain.

Elway again picks up the narrative. "We wanted to waste a

little more time and get it closer. We called a draw play that gained 10 yards. Now it was time for the field goal. I came to the sidelines and everybody was celebrating—hooting and hollering, and I'm thinking, hey, it's not over. We still have to make the field goal. I'm thinking of that missed extra point."

Elway's fears were almost prophetic. The snap was high, and when holder Gary Kubiak put the ball down, it was horizontal. He got it upright just as Treadwell's toe hit the ball. It sailed toward the upright but went through. Sixteen seconds remained, but Houston could do no more damage. Denver won 26–24.

Broncos 20, Chiefs 19
(October 4, 1992—Mile High Stadium)

There was no bigger nemesis to Marty Schottenheimer than Elway and the Broncos. It started at Cleveland with The Drive. Now at Kansas City, Marty was faring no better. This time Denver seemed out of it. At the two-minute warning the Broncos trailed 19–6. From the broadcast booth Dave Logan and I could see the crowd streaming to the parking lots. We warned them that with Elway, you could never count Denver out. No sooner had we said that than John launched a strike to Mark Jackson in the end zone. With 1:55 remaining the Broncos were within six points, and the stream of fans reversed itself and headed back to the stadium.

The Broncos defense made quick work of the Chiefs and the punt was returned 28 yards by Arthur Marshall to the Kansas City 27. Two plays later, the ball was at the Chief 12. Elway lofted a pass to the end zone that ended up in Vance Johnson's hands and the Broncos won 20–19.

Elway had done it again.

Chiefs 31, Broncos 28
(October 17, 1994–Mile High Stadium)

Before a *Monday Night Football* audience Elway and Schottenheimer were at it again. This time Marty had a gunslinger by the name of Joe Montana at his side. The Broncos took advantage of an errant Montana pass that ended up in an interception and scored the first touchdown. Montana came back with a touchdown drive climaxed by a 7-yard run by Marcus Allen. It was Elway's turn—a 27-yard scoring pass to Anthony Miller. Then it was Montana to J. J. Birden and the score was 14–14. A major drama was playing out as the teams went to the locker room.

Montana engineered a 76-yard drive to start the second half and went to his bag of tricks by passing to Joe Voleria, on a tackle-eligible play, for the go-ahead points. Elway came right back and hit a 20-yard pass to Jerry Evans to tie the game going into the final stanza.

Montana drove to the Bronco 1 before settling for a field goal. Denver seemed doomed with 2:45 to go and the Chiefs in possession at their 41, but sure-handed Marcus Allen fumbled, Karl Mecklenburg recovered, and six plays later, working out of the shotgun, Elway ran 6 yards for the touchdown, putting Denver ahead 24–21. Now 1:29 remained.

This fantastic game, matching two of the best quarterbacks in the game, wound down with Montana marching the Chiefs 75 yards in nine plays. His touchdown pass to Willie Davis with eight seconds remaining gave Kansas City the win.

Reflecting on the game, Elway said, "It was a great game. Joe made the plays. I guess we owed Marty at least one. I'm sure it was a great game to watch."

It was.

Broncos 31, Bears 29
(November 16, 1987 – Mile High Stadium)

It was another Monday night and the Bears were just two years removed from their Super Bowl championship. The Broncos had been to the Super Bowl the previous season. It was another classic quarterback match: Elway versus Jim McMahon.

McMahon put Chicago ahead 14–0. Elway got a touchdown back, and the Bears moved to the Denver 1. There was still a lot of football to be played, but what happened at this point defined the game.

William "The Refrigerator" Perry, the 300-plus-pound defensive lineman, was used by Coach Mike Ditka as a blocking fullback in goal-line situations during Chicago's championship season. It was designed to give Walter Payton a big bulldozer near the goal line. The plan worked to perfection and the unpredictable Ditka actually let the big guy carry the ball into the end zone a time or two. It made Perry a folk hero.

With the ball at the 1, Perry lumbered onto the field. The play called for a handoff to Payton. For some still unexplained reason, McMahon changed the play and gave the ball to Perry. The Fridge fumbled and the Broncos recovered and went on to a score that tied the game. Before the half ended, Denver made it twenty-one straight points and had the lead.

Chicago got back out in front, but the Broncos ended up winning the game. The turning point was the fumble on the goal line.

The Snow Bowl—Broncos 17, Packers 14
(October 14, 1984—Mile High Stadium)

The most memorable of Denver's "bad weather" games was witnessed by the nation on Monday Night Football. The weathermen described it as "The Perfect Storm." The snow started in early afternoon. By game time Mile High Stadium was a winter wonderland, with twenty-nine-degree temperatures and a wind strong enough that the storm was officially termed a blizzard. Green Bay had the ball first. On the first play from scrimmage, the ball was knocked loose; Steve Foley scooped it up and ran 22 yards for a touchdown. The Broncos kicked off again. Once again, on the first play from scrimmage, there was a fumble. Louis Wright picked it up and took it to the end zone. The Broncos led 14–0 in two plays and they hadn't had the ball. The game settled down and Packer quarterback Lynn Dickey had a fine game in terrible conditions. He completed twenty-seven passes for 371 yards and two touchdowns. The difference in the game turned out to be a

The Packer Broadcast Crew Made Someone Happy

The longtime play-by-play voice of the Green Bay Packers, Jim Irwin, and his broadcast crew made someone very happy after the "perfect storm" game. While Jim and his color commentator, Max McGee, were wrapping up the broadcast, some members of the broadcast crew headed to the parking lot to dig out their buried rental car. They were proud of the job they had done until Jim and Max arrived. They had dug out the wrong car and had to do it all over again.

Sammy Winder (23) gains yards against Green Bay in the famed Snow Bowl, played in a blizzard on Monday Night Football, on October 15, 1984. (Courtesy Rod Hanna/Rich Clarkson and Associates)

field goal by Denver's "barefoot" kicker, Rich Karlis. His teammates feared that he'd get frostbite, but he survived.

While on the subject of "bad weather" games, a couple of others deserve mention. On November 11, 1985, there was no snow during the game between the Broncos and 49ers, but there had been a considerable amount the day before. The field was clear, but the stands were full of snow. Predictably, some of the fans pelted the 49ers with snowballs. One particular snowball played a role in the outcome of the game. Denver led 17–16 as Ray Wershing set up for a short field goal that would give San Francisco the win on the final play of the game. As the kicker approached the ball, a snowball splattered near the pigskin, destroying Wershing's concentration. The kick fluttered wide and Denver won.

The coldest day for a Bronco game was on December 18, 1983, at Arrowhead Stadium in Kansas City. The wind chill was minus thirty degrees, yet 11,377 brave souls sat it out in the stands and enjoyed the Chiefs' 48–17 trouncing of Denver.

Broncos 30, Chargers 24
(November 17, 1985–Mile High Stadium)

Rich Karlis kicked a field goal to tie the game, 24–24, with five seconds to go. San Diego had the first possession in overtime and drove to the Denver 23. Bob Thomas lined up a 40-yard field-goal attempt, but Dennis Smith broke through the line and blocked it. Alas, it didn't count. One of the Broncos had called a time-out before the play and the block was not allowed. Thomas had another chance. Amazingly, Smith broke through the line and blocked it again. This time Louis Wright picked it up and ran 60 yards for a touchdown that won the game for Denver, with the Broncos offense never having the ball in the overtime period.

Seahawks 31, Broncos 27
(December 10, 1995–Mile High Stadium)

This was a memorable game because of Glyn Milburn, who didn't have a long or spectacular career as a Bronco, but had one memorable day. The Broncos running backs had been depleted and Milburn, primarily a punt returner and reserve receiver, was pressed into service as a running back. Milburn set an NFL record by gaining 404 all-purpose yards, which included rushing yards, pass receiving yards, and return yards, all in one game. However the Broncos blew a twenty-point lead and lost the game.

Oilers 45, Broncos 7
(September 3, 1966–Houston, Texas)

This season opener was the lowest point in Bronco history. Denver did not make a first down in the game. The only points came on an 88-yard kickoff return by Goldie Sellers.

Broncos 23, Raiders 23
(October 22, 1973–Mile High Stadium)

Broncos fans didn't like Howard Cosell. They lined up at sports bars to throw bricks at the television set when Howie was on the screen on *Monday Night Football.* Howard always had nasty things to say about the Broncos when he reviewed the games at halftime. Denver finally earned a spot on *Monday Night Football,* and the city was so excited about being part of prime time that it was almost a civic holiday. Mayor Bill McNichols hosted a luncheon attended by political and business leaders. Frank Gifford, Don Meredith, and Howie were treated like royalty. This was bigger than a presidential visit. It was proclaimed "Orange Monday." Mile High Stadium was a sea of orange and the Bronco fans were not disappointed.

The Raiders couldn't shake the Broncos as quarterback Charley Johnson made some big plays to keep them in the game. The task seemed insurmountable when George Blanda booted a field goal with forty-four seconds remaining. Johnson went to work and completed a pass to Floyd Little. Successive runs by Joe Dawkins and Little set up a 35-yard field goal attempt by Jim Turner. He kicked it between the uprights with seven seconds remaining. There was no overtime rule then, so the game ended 23–23, and it wasn't like kissing your sister. Broncos fans considered it a victory. The Raiders had won

Placekicker Jim Turner booted a field goal that gave Denver a 23–23 tie with Oakland in the Broncos' historic first Monday Night Football game on October 22, 1973. (Courtesy Rich Clarkson and Associates)

fourteen of the previous fifteen meetings, and it was the first time that Oakland hadn't won in Denver since 1964.

Turner fondly remembers the kick. "There was no way I'd miss that kick," he said, "It's a great memory."

Johnson, who was in the twilight of his career, which had many milestones in St. Louis and Houston, said, "I'll never forget it. It was the highlight of my career. It put the Broncos on the map and gave them respectability. What a thrill."

Broncos 37, Seahawks 34
(September 23, 1979–Mile High Stadium)

Bronco fans got accustomed to comebacks by number 7. In this game the number 7 was Craig Morton. John Elway was still a freshman at Stanford at this point in 1979.

It didn't seem to be Denver's day. Seattle built up a 34–10 lead and the starting quarterback who had taken the Broncos to the Super Bowl two seasons before was on the bench. Coach Red Miller called for Morton to go in the game. An angry Morton reluctantly joined the fray and led Denver to one of its greatest come-from-behind victories. He threw for three touchdowns in 1:19 and then engineered the game winner.

Rob Lytle scored the winning TD, went through the end zone, and handed the ball to Bob Peck, who was sitting in a wheelchair on the track in front of the South Stands. Peck was the long-time director of media relations, who was battling brain cancer. He would die shortly after that game.

Morton remembers: "To me that was the greatest moment in Bronco football. Peck was such a great guy, a Bronco institution, and Lytle had enough insight to know exactly what he wanted to do."

Veteran quarterback Craig Morton, who wore number 7 for the Broncos before John Elway, had a big comeback against Seattle in 1979.
(Courtesy Rich Clarkson and Associates)

AFC Championship Game—Broncos 20, Raiders 17
(January 1, 1978—Mile High Stadium)

The Broncos watched the clock run out to win their first AFC championship, touching off a Mile High celebration. It was a gutsy performance by quarterback Craig Morton, who couldn't even tie his shoelaces before the game. Morton put Denver up early with a 74-yard touchdown pass to Haven Moses and connected with him again in the fourth quarter on a 12-yard touchdown pass that gave the Broncos a 20–10 lead. Oakland

Why Was Craig Morton on the Bench?

Craig Morton's disputes with Coach Red Miller were legend.

On this particular day, Morton remembered: "Red was mad at me, so he benched me. It was one of those times when we weren't getting along too well. We were down by twenty-four points and Red told me to go in. I said, 'You're crazy, I'm not going in there.' When you're down by that much the quarterback is going to get killed, because all the defense does is come after you. Some of my teammates came over and urged me to get in the game. Red called a play out to me as I started on to the field. I needed to change the mood of the team, so when I got to the huddle, I asked them, 'Can you believe he called this play when we're behind?' It was an effort to get the players excited, so I changed the play. Everybody started laughing and I figured we would get something going. I told Rick Upchurch, 'Uppy, run down the field, I'm going to throw it to you.' I completed a screen pass for 15 yards. When we huddled again, I said, 'You see, this is easy.'"

Morton kept the drive going, ran for the touchdown, and things started to click. He passed for a touchdown to Haven Moses. He said, "All of a sudden things were happening. I could have thrown left-handed, behind my back, between my legs, and they would all be complete."

Morton made it 34–31 on a TD pass to Upchurch, all in 1:19.

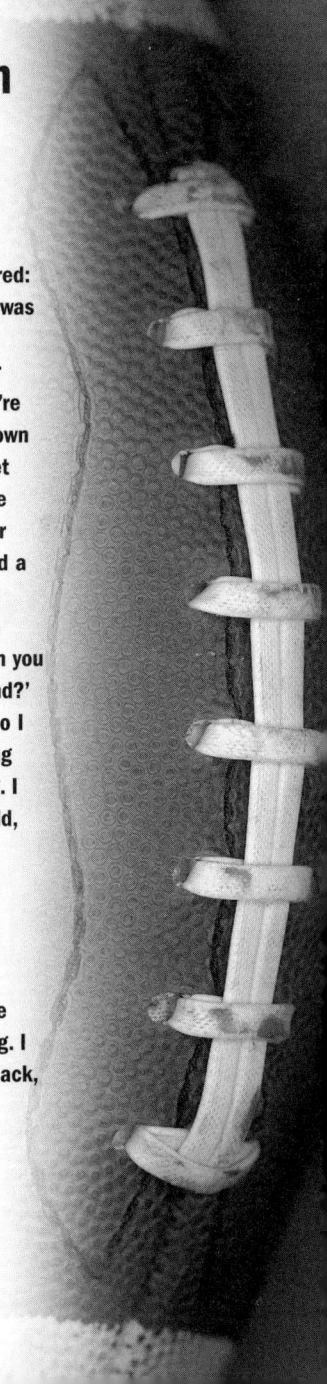

narrowed the margin to 20–17, but Morton engineered a couple of first downs to keep the ball away from the Raiders for the rest of the game.

AFC Playoffs–Broncos 34, Steelers 21
(December 24, 1977–Mile High Stadium)

It was the first playoff game in Denver's history. Pittsburgh's playoff-hardened team came to town intent on bursting the Broncos' bubble, but Craig Morton and Tom Jackson made big plays to give Denver its most important victory to date. It was a seesaw game that was tied three times, but the Broncos never trailed. Rob Lytle and Otis Armstrong had touchdown runs, and Morton threw touchdown passes to Riley Odoms and Jack Dolbin. Jim Turner added two field goals. With Terry Bradshaw, Franco Harris, Lynn Swann, and John Stallworth on the field for the Steelers, the Broncos were never comfortable until two fourth-quarter interceptions by linebacker Tom Jackson put the game out of reach.

Broncos 13, Patriots 10
(September 9, 1960–Boston University Field)

Because the Boston Patriots were playing at the Boston University Field and had to work around the University's schedule, the game ended up being played on Friday night. By this quirk of fate, this became the historic first game played in the American Football League. Denver was 0–5 in preseason, but they were ready for this game. Gene Mingo returned a punt 76 yards to provide the impetus to Denver's win.

About the Author

Larry Zimmer has been pursuing his dream of being a sportscaster since he was ten years old. He did his first broadcast, while in high school, on WJBO in Baton Rouge, Louisiana. He pursued a journalism degree at both Louisiana State University and the University of Missouri, graduating with a Bachelor of Journalism in 1957. After a two-year stint in the U.S. Army Artillery as a first lieutenant, he built the foundation of his play-by-play career at KFRU in Columbia, Missouri, broadcasting high school football and basketball.

In 1966 Zimmer moved to WAAM in Ann Arbor, Michigan, and was the football, basketball, and hockey announcer for the Wolverines. He moved to Denver and KOA Radio/TV in 1971 and is still there today. He worked as the color commentator on the Denver Broncos Network for nineteen years with Bob Martin. When Martin died, Zimmer took over the play-by-play duties through 1996. He broadcast his 500th Bronco game during the 1995 season. He has been the Voice of the Colorado Buffaloes football and basketball for thirty years.

Other highlights of Zimmer's career include broadcasting the Denver Rockets in the American Basketball Association, telecasts of regional college basketball on NBC, CBS, and ESPN, telecasts of North American Soccer League games, and numerous World Cup Ski Events. He was a member of the CBS Radio broadcast team for the 1980 Winter Olympics in Lake Placid. He also teaches a course in sports broadcasting at the University of Colorado School of Journalism and Mass Communications.

His awards include being named Colorado Sportscaster of the Year five times by the National Sportscasters and Sportswriters Association, Colorado Broadcaster of the Year in 1995, numerous awards for ski journalism, and he received the 2000 Powerade National Sports Story of the Year Award for his series "Mile High Memories."

Zimmer is an opera lover and an avid skier. He serves on the Board of Directors of Opera Colorado and the advisory board of the Colorado Ski Museum and Hall of Fame.

His name is included in *Who's Who in America.*